Welcome to the new year and to the first annual publication of **In Good Company: A Woman's Journal for Spiritual Reflection.**

We hope that throughout this coming year you will be in good company as you **journal** in response to women who have wisdom to share. Special thanks to the following friends and colleagues who submitted **quotations** to be included in this year's journal: K. C. Ackley, Lib Caldwell, Arthur Clyde, Hilda Davis, Joyce DeToni Hill, Linda Douty, Mitzi Eilts, Pat Goldberg, Sue Joiner, Jonathan McNair, Lydia Meyer, Helen Neinast, Kim Sadler, Donna Schaper, Ansley Coe Throckmorton, and Miriam Therese Winter. Special thanks to Martha Clark for her elegant design of the journal and to the photographers for their submissions.

May 1996 offer you new **insights** and a keen sense of **direction** as you continue your spiritual journey.

—LYNNE M. DEMING, PUBLISHER

Introduction

*or as long as I can remember, I have entrusted my innermost thoughts to a blank sheet of **paper.** Before I ever knew what a **journal** was or understood the value of chronicling the movements of the spirit, I recorded for keeps the highlights of my dialogue with the universe. There were never a lot of words, just snippets of **inspiration** that attempted to capture my intuitive struggle with the meaning of life here and hereafter, words that filled me with delight, connecting the limited world of my embodiment to the vast, mysterious, exciting world of my imagination.* ❧ *Looking back I would say that, as a little girl, I was a **philosopher** who grappled with theology, even as I do now. I suspect, however, that the little girl would respond otherwise. She would say that she liked to talk to birds and trees and wind and God, that she liked **writing** poems. I was often in conversation with the inner spirit of all living things. I was always writing poems.* ❧ *At the age of six I came to grips with the meaning of metaphor, the* power of **analogy,** the magic of **symbol** and **sound.** My first-grade teacher sensed that I knew far more than I could tell. She said, think about what you want to say, then put it down on paper. What I produced wasn't all that spectacular. It had something to do with pussy willows, just a line or two of ordinary stuff, with a flicker of insight within it. Yet I was thrilled with what I had **written,** for I knew it had drawn me to the threshold of an unseen universe, had put me in **touch** with a reality that would carry me back and forth in time, between this world and the world to come, between meaning and mystery. I had felt the power of **poetry** and been touched by the **wisdom** within the word. By the time I was midway through second grade, I had a whole pad full of poems.   🐚   I have always loved blank paper and its potential for **evoking** poetry, tranquillity, and prayer. I continue to relish notebooks and pads—the contemporary word is journal. I can't resist a journal, nor could I resist the invitation to write a word in this one. Journals for me are **magical,** and **secret,** and **sacred.** I can say what I want, say what I feel in ways that make sense to me, perhaps only to me. I am free to question, to explore, to reinvest, to reimagine. A journal, this journal, promises precious hours of prayerful introversion. It hints of new **discoveries** for the heart through a Spirit-led conversation with life inside and out and through conversation with other women. ❧ Nowadays I am continually **enriched** by the wisdom of women's experience embedded in the written word. An incisive **quote** from a favorite writer stimulates me to reflect, and connect, and in some way to respond. A treasury of women's wisdom exists within feminist publications, which form a vast body of literature that is growing every day. Since we haven't time to read everything, try as we might, the next best thing is to read little bits from a wide variety of sources. To a certain extent that helps us to know which way our world is going, puts us in touch with **essentials** during times of existential change. What a privilege it is to have access to words that flow from the heart of a sister as the fruit of her reflection or the result of her scholarship. It helps us to grow within ourselves and in relationship to one another. That is what journaling is about. ❧ This very special journal places us in **good company** and invites us into dialogue with a multitude of women struggling to prepare the way for a new, fully inclusive creation. Their words **echo** the truly good news of a world envisioned by Jesus, which one day will come to pass. Such a world already exists in spirit *whenever two or more dream **dreams** in which we dare to imagine ourselves as the Spirit's dwelling place. Write the vision down, says God, and bring it to birth together. How blessed are we to be traveling in the company of one another, **sharing** intuitive wisdom, **telling** our collective story, pushing back the boundaries that restrict or stifle grace.*

❧   *This journal encourages women to celebrate a common journey that is unfolding in new ways. It **invites** us to **write** what arises within, whether poetry or prose or prayer, and to enter into relationship with a spirit guide each day. However, do not be anxious if the dailiness seems intimidating because your schedule is so demanding or you just need time to think. So what if it happens to be July and you want to **respond** to a particular text that appeared in January. The world of the spirit teaches us to transcend limitations. Be free to be your true self here. That, after all, is what matters.   ❧   What is born of the spirit from deep within will continue in its own way. It may be that sometime in the future, something some one of us records here will enliven another **book** of days.   ❧*

— MIRIAM THERESE WINTER

Monday, January 1

NEW YEAR'S DAY

A bright new year
reminds us of God's promise.
—LAVON BAYLER

Tuesday, January 2

Fifteen minutes of silent listening
each morning can attune us to the
voice of creation throughout the day.
—MARIA HARRIS

Wednesday, January 3

One cannot understand feminist
theology as long as one believes
that it is simply a change of posi-
tion or an exchange of pronouns.

—DOROTHEE SÖLLE

Thursday, January 4

If we try to understand the past
and leave women out, we have
learned only a partial history.

—ANN J. LANE

Friday, January 5

Saturday, January 6

EPIPHANY

Sunday, January 7

Isaiah 42:1-9

Psalm 29

Acts 10:34-43

Matthew 3:13-17

My servant will not fail or be

discouraged till justice has been

established in the earth; and the

coastlands wait for the servant's law.

—Isaiah 42:4

Hierarchical systems prevail by making us feel inadequate and imperfect, whatever we do, so we will **internalize** *the blame. But once we realize there is no such thing as adequacy or perfection, it sets us* **free** *to say:* **We might as well be who we really are.**

—GLORIA STEINEM

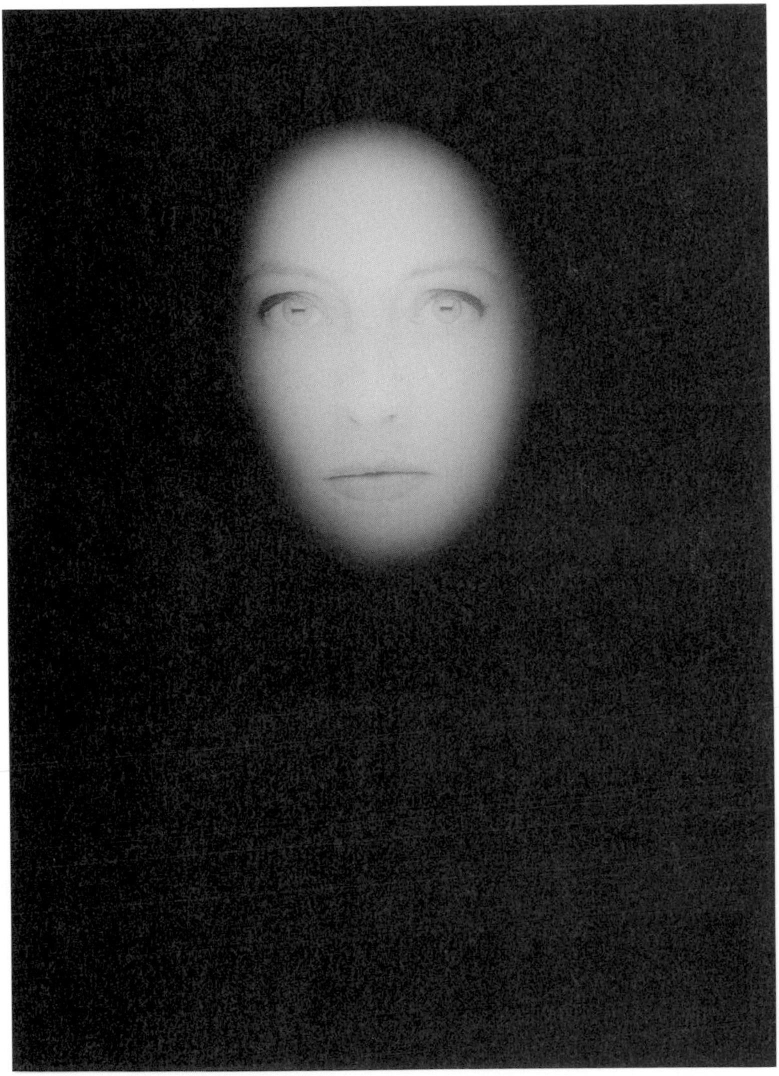

Vaccariello, *Elizabeth*, ©1991

Monday, January 8

*True sharing of power leads
to mutuality, and that is what we
Hispanic feminists ask
of Anglo feminists.*

—ADA MARÍA ISASI-DÍAZ

Tuesday, January 9

*So many of us structure our
private and public lives according to
biblical values that are not always
accurately portrayed.*

—MIRIAM THERESE WINTER

Wednesday, January 10

I don't want to be anything
special, I only want to try to be
true to that in me which seeks to
fulfill its promise.

—ETTY HILLESUM

Thursday, January 11

Women have had to learn, often
painfully and always with reluc-
tance, that their freedom will not
simply come of its own accord.

—ROSALIND MILES

Friday, January 12

How we speak to and about God matters.

—RUTH C. DUCK

Saturday, January 13

The eradication of gender
oppression cannot occur fully apart
from the eradication of race and
class oppression.

—MARCIA Y. RIGGS

Sunday, January 14

Isaiah **49**:**1**–**7**

Psalm **40**:**1**–**11**

1 Corinthians **1**:**1**–**9**

John **1**:**29**–**42**

God put a new song in my mouth,

a song of praise to our God.

—Psalm 40:3

*Therefore we must fearlessly **pull out** of ourselves and **look** at and **identify** with our lives the living creativity some of our great-grandmothers were not allowed to know.*

—ALICE WALKER

Amy Sorokas, Untitled, ©1994

Monday, January 15

MARTIN LUTHER KING JR. DAY

Black women serve as contemporary prophets, calling other[s] . . . [to] break away from the oppressive ideologies and belief systems that presume to define their reality.

—KATIE GENEVA CANNON

Tuesday, January 16

The ultimate aim of a feminist consciousness is to make the experience and insights of women available to the entire world.

—BARBARA BROWN ZIKMUND

Wednesday, January 17

*A woman must have money
and room of her own if she is to
write fiction.*
—VIRGINIA WOOLF

Thursday, January 18

*The search for theological imagery
is a journey whose destinations are
rarely apparent at the outset.*
—MARCIA FALK

Friday, January 19

_____
_____
_____
_____
_____
_____
_____

The emerging feminist paradigm
_____
trying to make sense of biblical and
_____
theological truth claims is
_____
*that of **authority as partnership.***
—LETTY M. RUSSELL

Saturday, January 20

_____
_____
_____
_____
_____
_____
_____
_____
_____

Our spiritual thirst gives birth
_____
to our faith.
—HELEN BRUCH PEARSON

Sunday, January 21

ISAIAH 9:1-4

PSALM 27:1, 4-9

1 CORINTHIANS 1:10-18

MATTHEW 4:12-23

I appeal to you, sisters and brothers, by the name of our Sovereign Jesus Christ, that all of you agree that there be no dissensions among you, but that you be united in the same mind and the same judgment.

—1 CORINTHIANS 1:10

To him handmade was always homemade, while to her **homemade** *was something you knew everything about, a contribution you made to your own* **history.**

—JANE SMILEY

Marilyn C. Szalay, *A Marriage of Elements*, ©1990

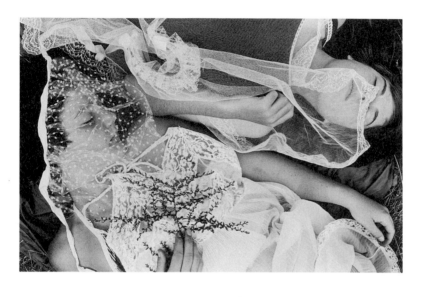

Monday, January 22

Of any stopping place in life, it is
good to ask whether it will be a
good place from which to go on as
well as a good place to remain.

—MARY CATHERINE BATESON

Tuesday, January 23

As truly as God is our Father,
so truly is God our Mother.

—JULIAN OF NORWICH

Wednesday, January 24

For women, the Christian message
is a feminist challenge to take
ourselves seriously as subjects of
our own lives.

—CARTER HEYWARD

Thursday, January 25

Communication is a continual
balancing act, juggling the
conflicting needs for intimacy
and independence.

—DEBORAH TANNEN

Friday, January 26

In the tender compassion of our
God the morning sun from heaven
will rise upon us.

—ELISE S. ESLINGER

Saturday, January 27

Weeping women, women whose
hearts moan like a flute because
those they love have come to harm,
are everywhere in the world.

—ELIZABETH A. JOHNSON

Sunday, January 28

MICAH 6:1-8

PSALM 15

1 CORINTHIANS 1:18-31

MATTHEW 5:1-12

Blessed are those who mourn,

for they shall be comforted.

—MATTHEW 5:4

*The **peace** that comes with claiming our self in God is the foundation of our ability to **carry** God's reconciling **love** to others in the most **humble** places and humble, everyday ways.*

—ROBERTA C. BONDI

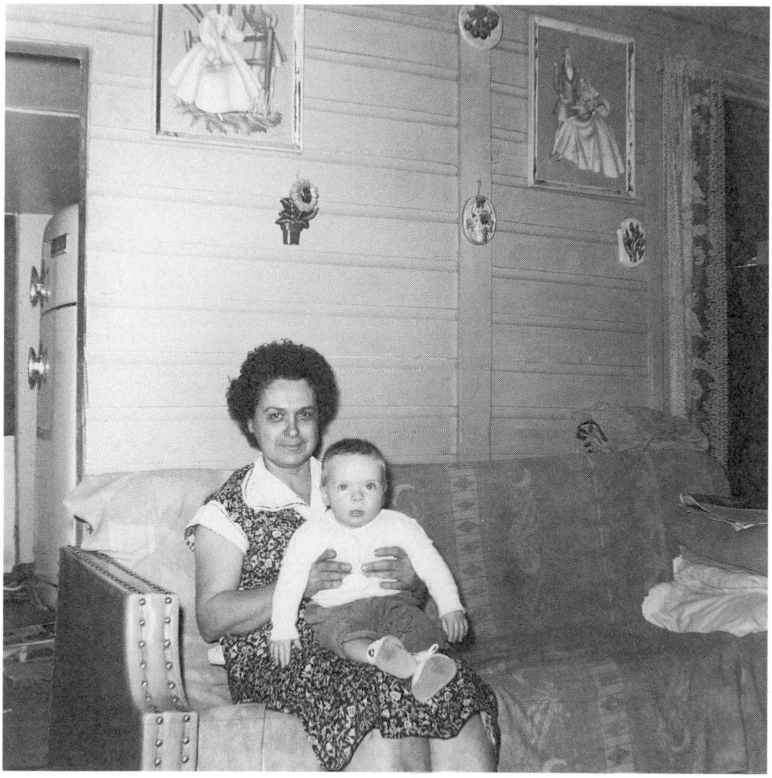

Thomas Jares, Grandmother/Granddaughter, ©1995

Monday, January 29

*Courage is crucial to putting the
past behind and moving with joy
toward an unknown future.*

—BARBARA BARKSDALE CLOWSE

Tuesday, January 30

*Black womanists are proposing a
decidedly inclusive perspective
that is acutely aware of the need
for the simultaneous liberation
from all oppression.*

—MARCIA Y. RIGGS

Wednesday, January 31

My purposes are the geography
that marks out my line of travel
toward the person I want to be.
—ALICE KOLLER

Thursday, February 1

An increasing number of women
recognize the need to create a new
ideology, to rewrite their
understanding of human life and of
society and their place in it.
—CARROLL SAUSSY

Friday, February 2

*Friendship, not coupledness, ought
to be the relational norm, especially
within the Christian tradition.*

—MARY E. HUNT

Saturday, February 3

*Our progress in holiness depends
on God and ourselves.*

—MOTHER TERESA

Sunday, February 4

ISAIAH 58:1-9A (9B-12)

PSALM 112:1-9 (10)

1 CORINTHIANS 2:1-12 (13-16)

MATTHEW 5:13-20

*God is gracious, merciful,
and righteous.*

—PSALM 112:4B

Joy sinks far deeper into one's being and dwells there much like the easy **purring** of a reliable car engine, aware of but unperturbed by bad weather. *Joy anchors* itself deeply, establishes roots, and endures in the worst circumstances alongside an **unconquerable** gladness that no barrier can confine.

—DORIS DONNELLY

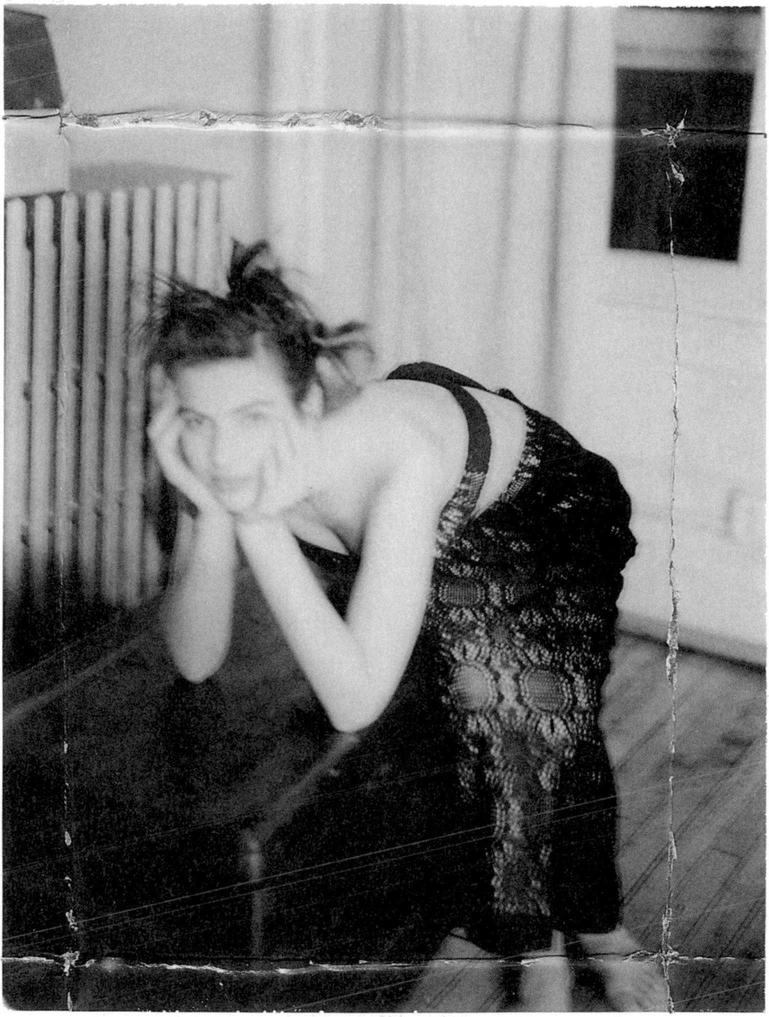

Jerry Mann, Untitled, ©1989

Monday, February 5

*Where does the biblical understanding
of hospitality as a moral obligation fit
into our busy lives?*

—Sara Covin Juengst

Tuesday, February 6

*Jewish and Christian feminists are
questioning many of the presuppositions
undergirding conceptual models
traditionally used by biblical scholars to
illumine the world of ancient Israel.*

—Katheryn Pfisterer Darr

Wednesday, February 7

If we show compassion, it is because
we have been shown compassion.

—BARBARA BROWN TAYLOR

Thursday, February 8

The images and metaphors we use
to talk about God are necessarily
culturally conditioned, and
biblical ones are no exception.

—KWOK PUI-LAN

Friday, February 9

*Courage is not synonymous
with fearlessness. On the contrary,
it often means taking necessary
action while afraid.*

—BARBARA BARKSDALE CLOWSE

Saturday, February 10

*When women are admitted to jobs
that heretofore only men have
filled, they must not be expected to
do the job in the same old way.*

—ANN BELFORD ULANOV

Sunday, February 11

DEUTERONOMY 30:15–20

PSALM 119:1–8

1 CORINTHIANS 3:1–9

MATTHEW 5:21–37

So neither the one who plants nor

the one who waters is anything, but

only God who gives the growth.

—1 CORINTHIANS 3:7

*There is another **garden** inherited from my mother that I consider even more significant. It is the **garden** where **love** and the **joy** of life flourish. It is the garden remembered even by her **grandchildren,** who knew her only when they were very young. . . . Her life was not easy, but she was always **life-affirming.***

—JOANN NASH EAKIN

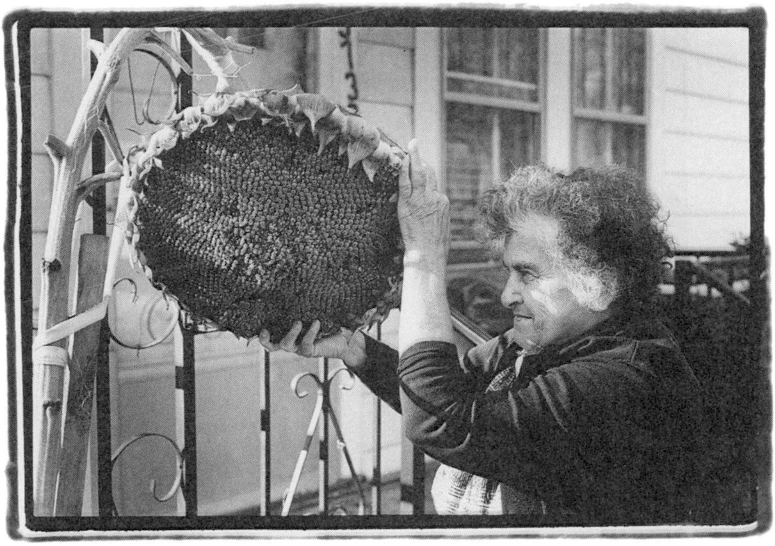

Thomas Jares, Auntie, ©1995

Monday, February 12

*Storytelling is a trinitarian act
that unites writer, text, and reader
in a collage of understanding.*

—PHYLLIS TRIBLE

Tuesday, February 13

*Women's religious protest and
affirmation can indeed be understood
as a grace for our times.*

—ANNE E. CARR

Wednesday, February 14

VALENTINE'S DAY

*Forgiveness constitutes a decision
to call forth and rebuild that love
which is the only authentic ground
of any human relationship.*

—MARJORIE J. THOMPSON

Thursday, February 15

*In the end Holy Wisdom is mystery
beyond all telling. Speaking about
God as mother points to the depth
of that absolute mystery.*

—ELIZABETH A. JOHNSON

Friday, February 16

*Prayer is meant to be not only
intensely relational but also
intensely practical. Expect, with
confidence, guidance to be given.*

—FLORA SLOSSON WUELLNER

Saturday, February 17

*Every generation must reinterpret
scripture anew, and that
reinterpretation includes weighing
the value of scriptural texts.*

—CHRISTINE E. GUDORF

Sunday, February 18

EXODUS 24:12–18

PSALM 2 (PSALM 99)

2 PETER 1:16–21

MATTHEW 17:1–9

First of all you must understand

this, that no prophecy of scripture is

a matter of one's own interpretation,

because no prophecy ever came by

human impulse, but people moved by

the Holy Spirit spoke from God.

—2 PETER 1:20–21

*Existential courage . . . is the courage to **see** and to **be** in the **face** of the nameless anxieties that surface when a woman begins to **see through** the **masks** of sexist society and to confront the horrifying fact of her own alienation from her authentic self.*

—MARY DALY

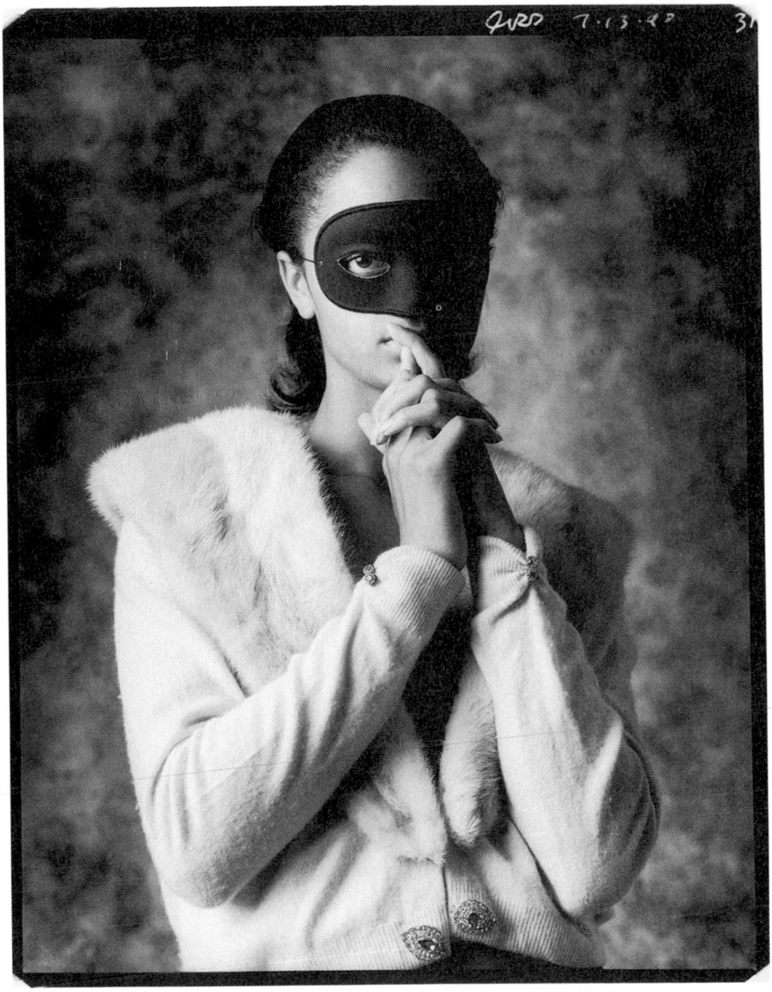

Geoffrey Pankhurst, Mask, ©1995

Monday, February 19

PRESIDENTS' DAY

*Women were not marginal figures
in [the early church] community
but exercised leadership as apostles,
prophets, and missionaries.*
—ELISABETH SCHÜSSLER FIORENZA

Tuesday, February 20

*At the beginning of the lenten season
we seek for ourselves those disciplines
of body, mind, and spirit that
will help us embrace the reconciling
ministry of Christ as our own.*
—LAVON BAYLER

Wednesday, February 21

*Christian feminists . . . must
address themselves to the
authority of the Bible in the life
of their community of faith.*
—KATHERINE DOOB SAKENFELD

Thursday, February 22

*Now God has built the human form
into the world structure, indeed even
the cosmos, just as an artist would
use a particular pattern in her work.*
—HILDEGARD OF BINGEN

Friday, February 23

Our God is a creative God. You are made in God's image and likeness. God wants you to be creative. Your relationship with God can then continually deepen and grow.

—VIRGINIA ANN FROEHLE

Saturday, February 24

Visiting the Garden of Eden in the days of the Women's Movement, we need no longer accept the traditional exegesis of Genesis 2–3.

—PHYLLIS TRIBLE

Sunday, February 25

GENESIS 2:15-17, 3:1-7

PSALM 32

ROMANS 5:12-19

MATTHEW 4:1-11

So when the woman saw that the

tree was good for food, and that it

was a delight to the eyes, and that the

tree was to be desired to make one

wise, she took of its fruit and ate.

—GENESIS 3:6

Eve's dilemma: a choice between obedience and knowledge. Between renunciation and appetite. Between subordination and desire. Between security and risk. Between loyalty and self-development. Between submission and power. Between hunger as temptation and hunger as vision. It is the **dilemma** of **modern women.**

—KIM CHERNIN

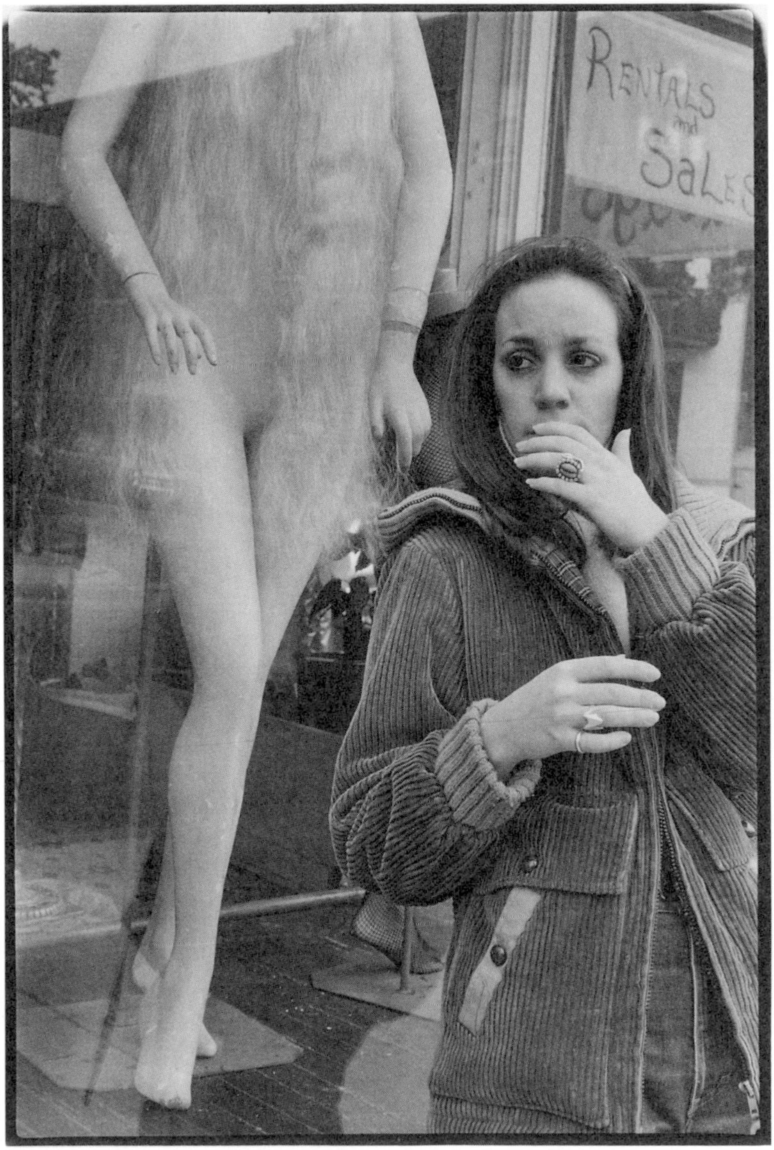
RENTALS
and
SALES

Marilyn C. Szalay, *Identity*, ©1984

Monday, February 26

*Groups concerned about a broad
range of gender, environment, and
development issues are seeking new
ways to harness the power of women
everywhere in creating change.*

—JODI L. JACOBSON

Tuesday, February 27

*Throughout its whole history, the
church has been in a process of
forgetting all feminine ways of talking
about God and enshrining the golden
calves of patriarchalimages of God.*

—RUTH C. DUCK

Wednesday, February 28

Our strength is made manifest
in struggle.
—DONNA SCHAPER

Thursday, February 29

There is nothing more unscriptural
and more opposed to the principles
of the New Testament than
discrimination between the sexes
in both Church and State.
—ALMA WHITE

Friday, March 1

*We are educated by the time
we spend alone in the company
of the Divine.*
—MARIA HARRIS

Saturday, March 2

*Love and anger are both
emotions of the free will, yet
only love is acceptable for the
powerless to express.*
—GLORIA STEINEM

Sunday, March 8

GENESIS 12:1-4A

PSALM 121

ROMANS 4:1-5, 13-17

JOHN 3:1-17 (MATTHEW 17:1-9)

I lift up my eyes to the hills.

From whence does my help come?

My help comes from God

who made heaven and earth.

—PSALM 121:1–2

*Often **without name** or **voice,** the women in the Gospels had **convictions** about Jesus and a security in him that **surpassed** that of the disciples, who were called by name and given a voice of great authority.*

—HELEN BRUCH PEARSON

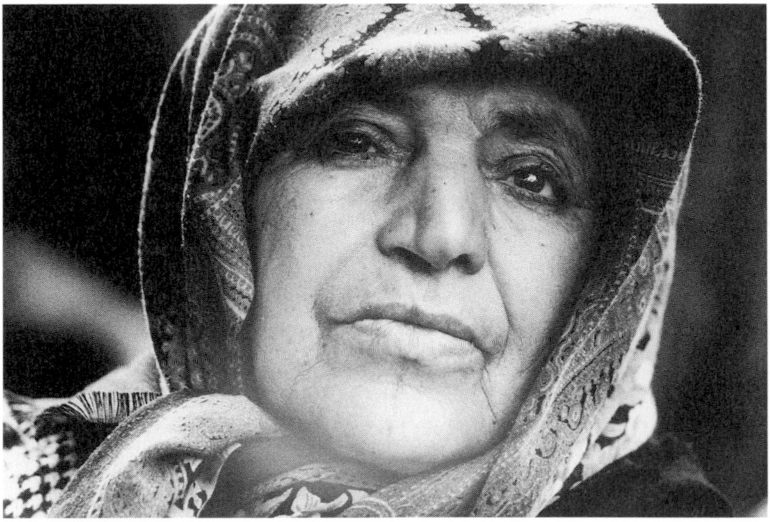

Luke Golobitsh, North African Woman, ©1993

Monday, March 4

You're lucky to be a girl.
Men are really unlucky;
they have a hard time just living.

—JANET KAUFFMAN

Tuesday, March 5

When we are filled with joy over
God's creation, we long to dance
with God and wonder who placed
that longing in our hearts.

—ELAINE M. WARD

Wednesday, March 6

*Women have traditionally cultivated a
communal personhood that could
participate in the successes of others
rather than seeing these as merely a
threat to one's own success.*

—ROSEMARY RADFORD RUETHER

Thursday, March 7

*This is a time of history when
each woman counts in the struggle
for recognition of who she is.*

—DIANA TREBBI

Friday, March 8

Faith can be known only by living it.

—CHRISTINE NELSON

Saturday, March 9

Today we would call Jesus a feminist, that is, a person who believes in the full personhood and equality of women and who acts to bring that belief to realization in society and church.

—SANDRA M. SCHNEIDERS

Sunday, March 10

THIRD   SUNDAY   IN   LENT

EXODUS 17:1–7

PSALM 95

ROMANS 5:1–11

JOHN 4:5–42

[The disciples] marveled that Jesus
was talking with a woman, but
none said, "What do you wish?"
or, "Why are you talking with
her?" So the woman left her water
jar, and went away into the city,
and said to the people, "Come, see
someone who told me all that I ever
did. Can this be the Christ?"

—JOHN 4:27–29

*Do we not love and fear the **freshness** of those who call us to **live** rather than to **stagnate,** to grow into our full spiritual stature rather than to settle for a **shallow** mediocrity of ourselves?*

—CARTER HEYWARD

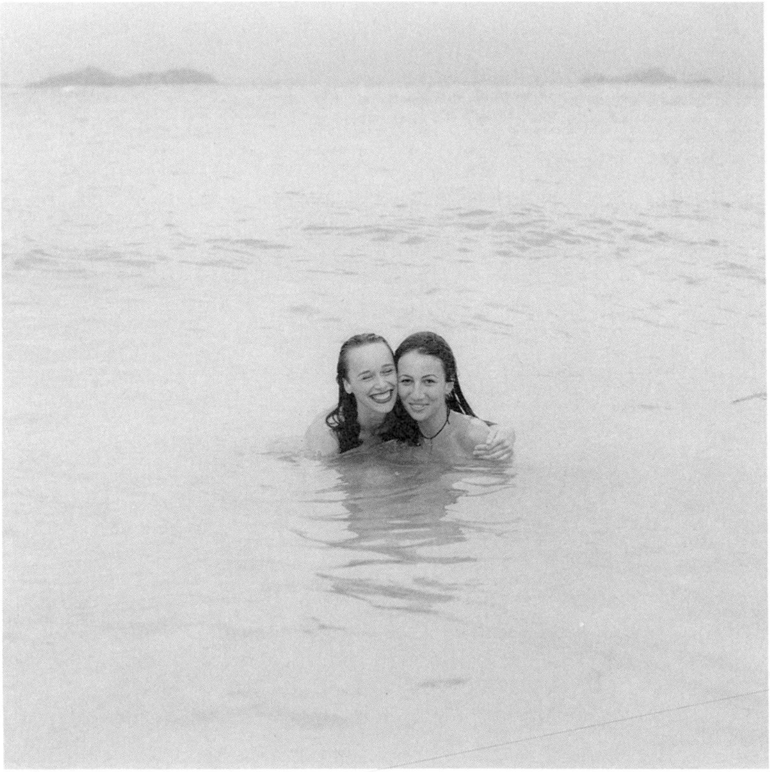

Donald Lesko, Untitled, ©1994

Monday, March 11

*The sisterhood model is inherently
one of equality and mutuality.*

—MARY ZIMMER

Tuesday, March 12

*The only certainties about what is
right and wrong are those which spring
from sources deep inside oneself.*

—ETTY HILLESUM

Wednesday, March 13

*As far as possible I only read what
I am hungry for at the moment
when I have an appetite for it, and
then I do not read, I* **eat.**

— SIMONE WEIL

Thursday, March 14

*By being a good representation, we
can become transparent people
through whom God's creative and
caring presence can shine.*

—CATHARINA J. M. HALKES

Friday, March 15

Women need to be more involved in the study and interpretation of their religious scriptures and tradition.

—MARIE ASSAAD

Saturday, March 16

There is no greater joy than meeting . . . other saints, other pilgrims, other traveling companions possessed of the same holy restlessness.

—HARRIET E. CROSBY

Sunday, March 17

FOURTH SUNDAY IN LENT

1 SAMUEL 16:1–13

PSALM 23

EPHESIANS 5:8–14

JOHN 9:1–41

*For once you were stumbling in the
night, but now you are light in the
Sovereign; walk as children of light.*

—EPHESIANS 5:8

*If we refuse to **engage** our pain, struggle, and uncertainty, we cut ourselves off both from the presence of God within those difficult times and from the possibility of new life emerging from them. By **acknowledging** our **struggles,** we **embrace** all of life and open ourselves to God in every moment.*

—JEAN M. BLOMQUIST

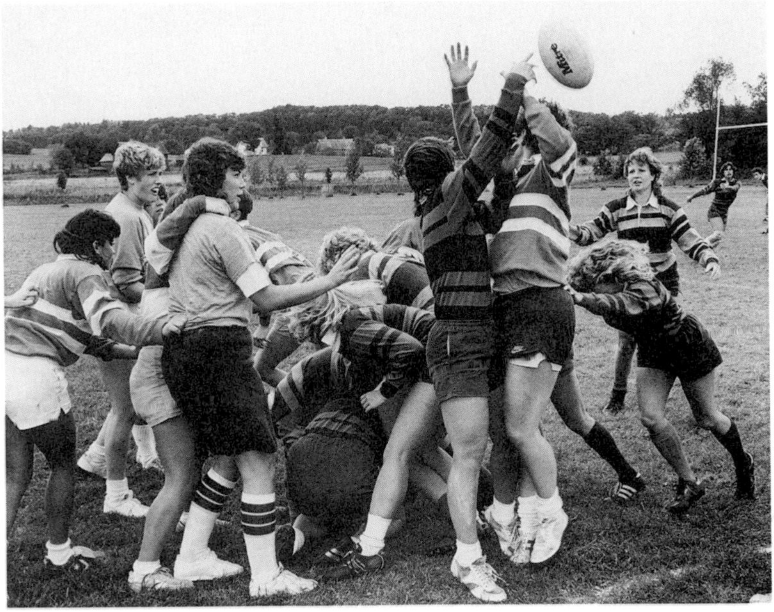

Bob Meier, Women Playing Football, ©1995

Monday, March 18

Christian belief must always be a process of coming to belief— like a story—through the ordinary details of historical life.

—SALLIE MCFAGUE

Tuesday, March 19

*There is a hunger for feminist theological reflection on the major symbols of Christian faith **from within the context of faith.***

—ANNE E. CARR

Wednesday, March 20

*Since the Spirit not only makes
human beings friends of God but
herself befriends the world, she can
rightly be named friend par excellence.*
—ELIZABETH A. JOHNSON

Thursday, March 21

*The God who calls me to begin
this journey of transformation is
the God who has the power to
work that transformation in me.*
—JUDITH E. SMITH

Friday, March 22

> Women working together are living
> examples of a community of knowers
> creating new being and new ways
> of acting through our conversations,
> through telling and retelling stories.
>
> —CAROL P. CHRIST

Saturday, March 23

> Attention. Deep listening. People
> are dying in spirit for lack of it.
>
> —MARY ROSE O'REILLEY

Sunday, March 24

EZEKIEL 37:1-14

PSALM 130

ROMANS 8:6-11

JOHN 11:1-45

[Martha] said to Jesus, "Yes,
Sovereign, I believe that you are
the Christ, the Child of God, the
one who is coming into the world."

—JOHN 11:27

Composing a life through memory as well as through day-to-day **choices** *. . . seems to me most essential to creative living. The past empowers the present, and the groping* **footsteps** *leading to this present* **mark** *the* **pathways** *to the future.*

—MARY CATHERINE BATESON

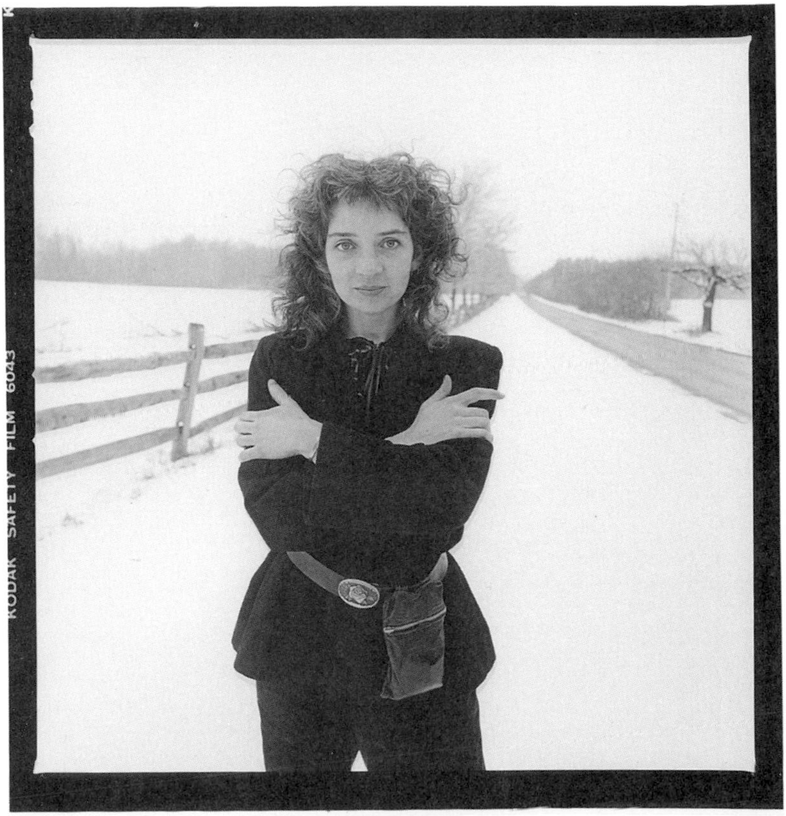
KODAK SAFETY FILM 6043

Geoffrey Pankhurst, Cindy, ©1995

Monday, March 25

The search for symbols seems to take the form of a "no-saying" and a "yes-saying" in which we see both the no and the yes as positive.

—NELLE MORTON

Tuesday, March 26

There is at work among women today a powerful religious force which cannot be fully explained in Christian terminology.

—SHEILA COLLINS

Wednesday, March 27

_Each one of us is unique and
therefore irreplaceable. And so
we must recognize the uniqueness
that is each one of us._

—MARY MCGEE

Thursday, March 28

_Our visions for a new heaven, new
earth, new society, new church, new
relations between the sexes, between
nations, between classes of peoples—
we know that these themselves await
a deeper liberation._

—MAUREEN P. CARROLL

Friday, March 29

See, you don't have to think
about doing the right thing.
If you're for the right thing,
then you do it without thinking.

—MAYA ANGELOU

Saturday, March 30

Faith cannot exist without its
shadow, doubt.

—DOROTHEE SÖLLE

Sunday, March 31

MATTHEW 21:1-11/ISAIAH 50:4-9A

PSALM 118:1-2, 19-29/PSALM 31:9-16

PHILIPPIANS 2:5-11

MATTHEW 26:14-27:66 (MATTHEW 27:11-54)

For the Sovereign God helps me;

  therefore I have not been confounded;

therefore I have set my face like a flint,

  and I know that I shall not be put to shame.

—ISAIAH 50:7

*We know something of the **wideness** of God's promise through the longings of our own **hearts** and through **moments** of graced encounter with one another.*

—WENDY M. WRIGHT

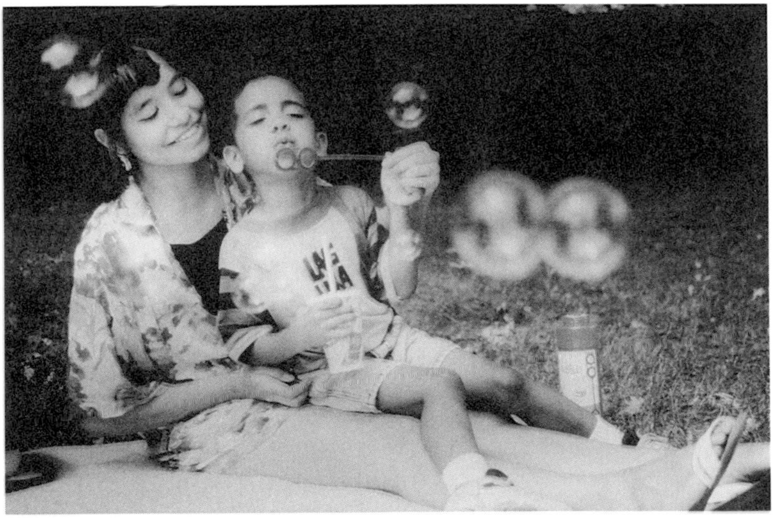

CLEO, *Untitled*, ©1995

Monday, April 1

*Suffering can bring enlightenment,
patience, and increased knowledge
of God, for God is indeed at the
edge of survival.*

—EUGENIA LEE HANCOCK

Tuesday, April 2

*The essential biblical message . . .
is not the sanctity of patriarchy
but the liberation of men and
women to relatedness with God.*

—PHYLLIS TRIBLE AND
ELISABETH FIORENZA

Wednesday, April 3

As we travel together on this
crystalline vessel called earth, I
wonder if the eyes of heaven do
not look to us for illumination.
—YVONNE V. SCHAUDT

Thursday, April 4

MAUNDY THURSDAY

The discerning Christian understands
that: Suffering is not a compound
sentence. Suffering is real.
—DIANE TENNIS

Friday, April 5

The brutal realities of crucifixion can feel much more real to us than the realities of resurrection.

—MARJORIE J. THOMPSON

Saturday, April 6

The cross reminds us that disaster is a possibility from which no one is immune.

—DONNA SCHAPER

Sunday, April 7

ACTS 10:34-43 (JEREMIAH 31:1-6)

PSALM 118:1-2, 14-24

COLOSSIANS 3:1-4 (ACTS 10:34-43)

JOHN 20:1-18 (MATTHEW 28:1-10)

Now on the first day of the week

Mary Magdalene came to the tomb

early, while it was still dark, and

saw that the stone had been taken

away from the tomb.

—JOHN 20:1

*[The resurrection] is God's presence among us, God's redeem-ing, **liberating** and blessing presence **in** this our world. God's world becomes God's **self-expression,** the sacrament through which the divinity expresses **her presence.***

—CATHARINA J. M. HALKES

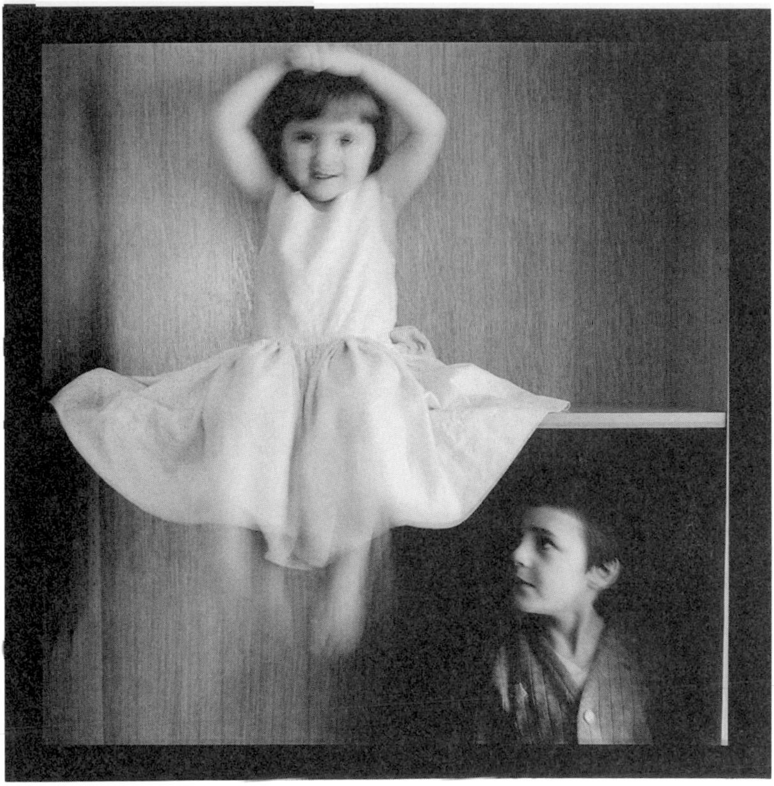

Geoffrey Pankhurst, Julia and Seth, ©1995

Monday, April 8

Occasionally, when you are not expecting it, something is awakened within you and you must connect to the God-presence in this world.
—SHARON BLESSUM SAWATZKY

Tuesday, April 9

*Throughout recorded history, women have tended to be **invisible** members of the Body of Christ, just as they and their experience have tended to be invisible in secular history.*
—NANETTE M. ROBERTS

Wednesday, April 10

To acknowledge that which we
cannot see, to give definition to
that which we do not know, to
create divine order out of chaos,
is the religious dance.

—TERRY TEMPEST WILLIAMS

Thursday, April 11

Life is trivia, but it is
through trivia that we glimpse
life's larger meanings.

—GRACIA GRINDAL

Friday, April 12

Saturday, April 13

Sunday, April 14

ACTS 2:14A, 22-32

PSALM 16

1 PETER 1:3-9

JOHN 20:19-31

You have made known to me the ways of life;

you will make me full of gladness with your presence.

—ACTS 2:28

*A **friend** is one whose presence is joy, ever-deepening relationship and love, ever available in direct address, in communion and presence. A **friend** is one who remains fundamentally a mystery, inexhaustible, never fully known, always surprising. Yet a **friend** is familiar, comforting, at home.*

—ANNE E. CARR

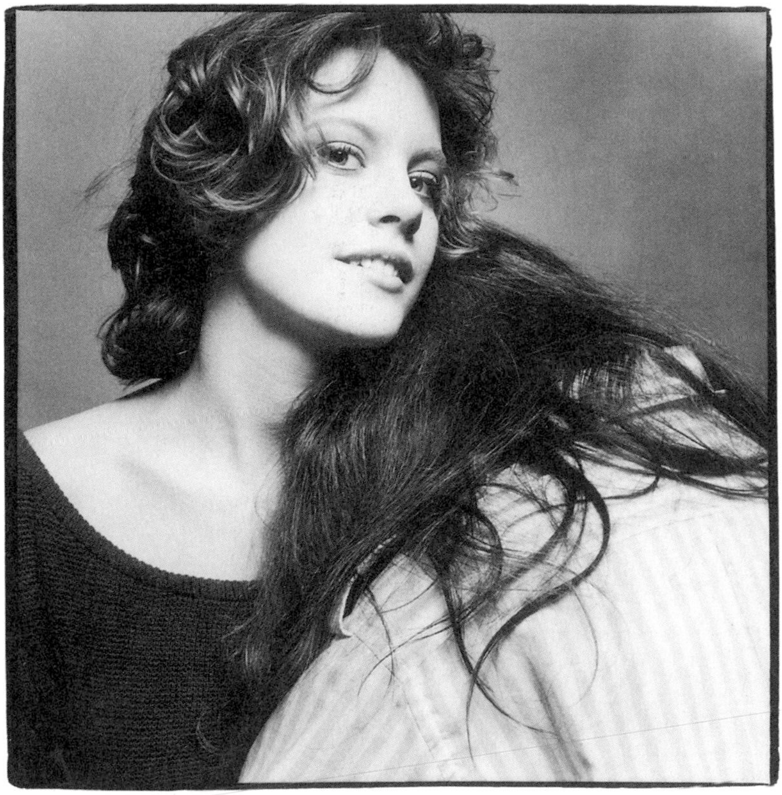

Jerry Mann, Untitled, ©1985

Monday, April 15

*Liturgy only gives sanction to
what the heart already knows.*
—PHYLLIS A. TICKLE

Tuesday, April 16

*When a proposal is turned
down or a job not offered, women
tend to say, I wasn't worthy.
Men more often contend that the
process was crooked.*
—MARY CATHERINE BATESON

Wednesday, April 17

Story and narrative theologizing
represent a powerful and
important way of naming reality
for women, and naming is clearly
a critical feminist issue.
—CHRISTINE M. SMITH

Thursday, April 18

To talk about religion in
some sense is to practice it.
—LYNDA SEXSON

Friday, April 19

To use female language in naming
the incomprehensible Deity makes
more available a perception of the
fullness of the mystery of God.

—CARROLL SAUSSY

Saturday, April 20

Above all else a feminist moral
theology insists that relationality is
at the heart of all things.

—BEVERLY WILDUNG HARRISON

Sunday, April 21

Acts 2:14a, 36–41

Psalm 116:1–4, 12–19

1 Peter 1:17–23

Luke 24:13–35

Moreover, some women of our company
amazed us. They were at the tomb
early in the morning and did not find
Jesus' body; and they came back saying
that they had even seen a vision of
angels, who said that Jesus was alive.

—Luke 24:22–23

*Genuine **friends,** whether of the **same** or **different** sex, age, race, or class, whether married to each other or not, whether family members, neighbors, professional colleagues, or any of the myriad combinations possible to human friendship, dwell within each other, in each other's **hearts** and **minds** and **lives.***

—ELIZABETH A. JOHNSON

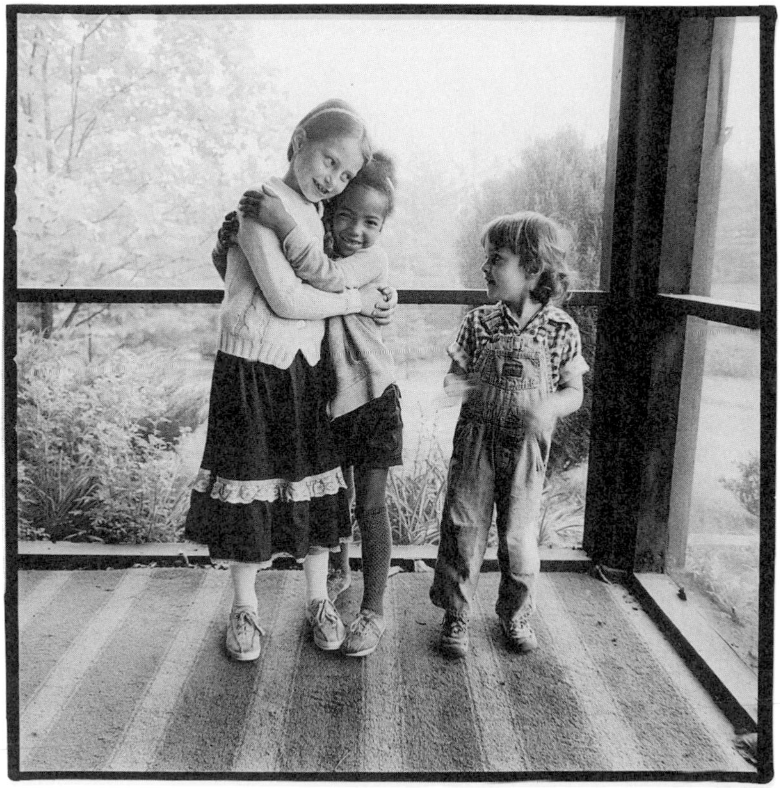

Geoffrey Pankhurst, Untitled, ©1995

Monday, April 22

*New interpretations of the concept
and reality of God . . . offer women a
theological ground for their deepest
struggle and for their final Christian
peace and security in that struggle.*

—ANNE E. CARR

Tuesday, April 23

*What would it mean to
truly seek God as the center of
my day-to-day existence?*

—JUDITH E. SMITH

Wednesday, April 24

The womanist perspective has as a
fundamental guiding premise a
principle of collective solidarity.

—MARCIA Y. RIGGS

Thursday, April 25

Spiritual disciplines are not a
system of working our way to
heaven. Rather, they are pathways
into the presence of God.

—WENDY MILLER

Friday, April 26

Saturday, April 27

Sunday, April 28

ACTS 2:42-47

PSALM 23

1 PETER 2:19-25

JOHN 10:1-10

And they devoted themselves to the teaching of the apostles and to community life, to the breaking of bread and to the prayers.

—ACTS 2:42

*To tell and hear tales of terror is to **wrestle demons** in the **night,** without a compassionate God to save us. . . . The fight itself is **solitary** and **intense.** We struggle mightily, only to be wounded. But yet we **hold on,** seeking a blessing: the healing of wounds and the restoration of health.*

—PHYLLIS TRIBLE

Marilyn C. Szalay, *The World Turns as We Sleep*, ©1992

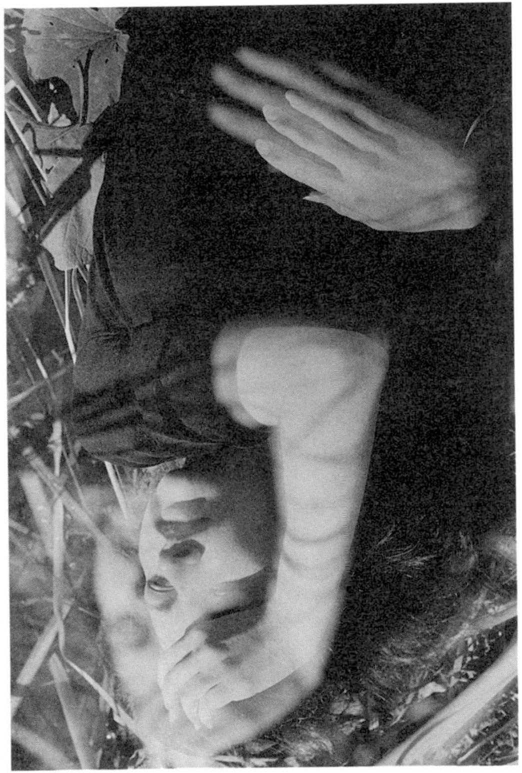

Monday, April 29

God is calling us each day to
renew the world—not by a blood-
and-thunder revolution, but by a
revolution in the hearts of people.
—TERRY WERTH

Tuesday, April 30

The meaning of our life and its
renewal are dependent on our faith
symbols and stories.
—ELAINE M. WARD

Wednesday, May 1

*Are we willing to let our perceptions
be cleansed so that we can
recognize our oneness with the whole
family of humankind?*

—Virginia Ramey Mollenkott

Thursday, May 2

*Do you ever feel that sense of
endless, hopeless, grinding effort in
your life—that a good portion of
your life consists largely in rolling
a huge stone uphill?*

—Jamie R. Gustafson

Friday, May 3

As every person is a creation
of God's own image, whose whole
self is sacred and precious, **any**
physical assault on a person
contradicts the very image of God.

—MARIE M. FORTUNE

Saturday, May 4

Women of faith . . . have been
moving in the direction of a new
and personal assumption of
responsibility in their desire to
respond to God's fractured creation.

—SALLY CUNNEEN

Sunday, May 5

Once you were no people but now

you are God's people; once you had

not received mercy but now you

have received mercy.

—1 PETER 2:10

*I believe that the **liberation** of the **human spirit** from her captivity, the **liberation of women,** and the **liberation** of the **oppressed** of the earth will come at one and the same time and be the same radical **movement** that will make a universal, visible reality and unify the spiritual and the political.*

—NELLE MORTON

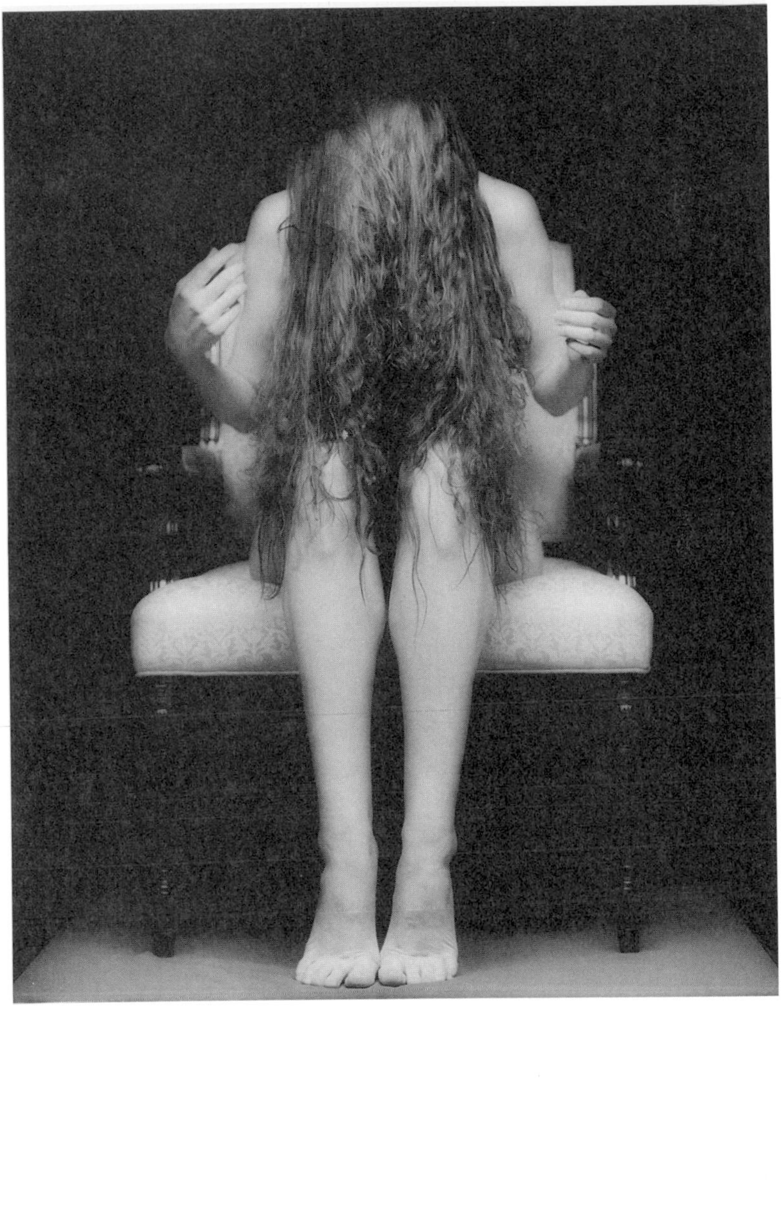

Vaccariello, *Deidre in Chair*, ©1993

Monday, May 6

> Women, in contrast [to men],
> tended to speak of themselves as
> living in connection with others.
> —LYN MIKEL BROWN
> AND CAROL GILLIGAN

Tuesday, May 7

> The lesson each of us has drawn
> from multiple fresh starts is
> that there is always something
> in the past to work with.
> —MARY CATHERINE BATESON

Wednesday, May 8

There have been countless great and deep friendships among women.

—MARY DALY

Thursday, May 9

I see a society in which everyone has enough to eat and to wear and is able to do what is individually fulfilling and what furthers the good of all.

—ELEANOR H. HANEY

Friday, May 10

The metaphor of mother and baby
illustrates the extravagant nature of
God's love for us.

—ROBERTA C. BONDI

Saturday, May 11

Those we consider to be members of
our family are, for us, gifts from
God. Through these everyday,
ordinary relationships, we meet God.

—ANNE BROYLES

Sunday, May 12

ACTS 17:22-31

PSALM 66:8-20

1 PETER 3:13-22

JOHN 14:15-21

Whoever has my commandments and

keeps them, that is the one who loves

me; and all who love me will be

loved by God, and I will love them

and manifest myself to them.

—JOHN 14:21

*Women have **worked**, constantly, continuously, always and everywhere, in every type of **society** in every part of the **world** since the beginning of human **time**.*

—HEATHER GORDON CREMONESI

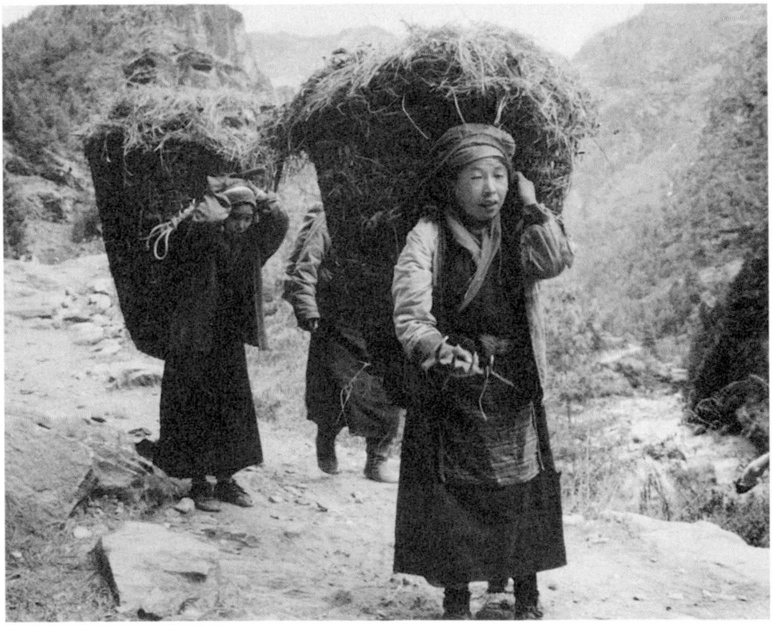

Ian Naysmith, Sherpa Women, ©1983

Monday, May 13

For a long time I have held my peace,
I have kept still and restrained
myself; now I will cry out like a
woman in labor, I will gasp and pant.

—ISAIAH 42:14

Tuesday, May 14

This is the work I do uninterruptedly
until I die, this work for women,
whom I love.

—SONIA JOHNSON

Wednesday, May 15

"Doing peace" is more like breathing:
You breathe today even
though you breathed yesterday.
—SUE NICHOLS SPENCER

Thursday, May 16

ASCENSION DAY

There is something about us
human beings that wants to hurt
or destroy the truly good.
—MARGIE M. FRANK

Friday, May 17

The song of Deborah . . . is a song of
courage and power. A song of women
interpreting the will of God, risking
their lives to do the will of God.

—PRISCILLA L. DENHAM

Saturday, May 18

A great artist . . . is never poor.
We have something . . . of which
other people know nothing.

—ISAK DINESEN

Sunday, May 19

ACTS 1:6-14

PSALM 68:1-10, 32-35

1 PETER 4:12-14, 5:6-11

JOHN 17:1-11

All these with one accord devoted

themselves to prayer, together with

the women and Mary the mother of

Jesus, and with Jesus' brothers.

—ACTS 1:14

Examine all things *intensely* and *relentlessly.* Probe and search each object in a piece of art. Do not leave it, do not course over it . . . but instead ***follow it*** down until you ***see it*** in the mystery of its own specificity and strength.

—ANNIE DILLARD

Marilyn C. Szalay, *Morning Friends*, ©1992

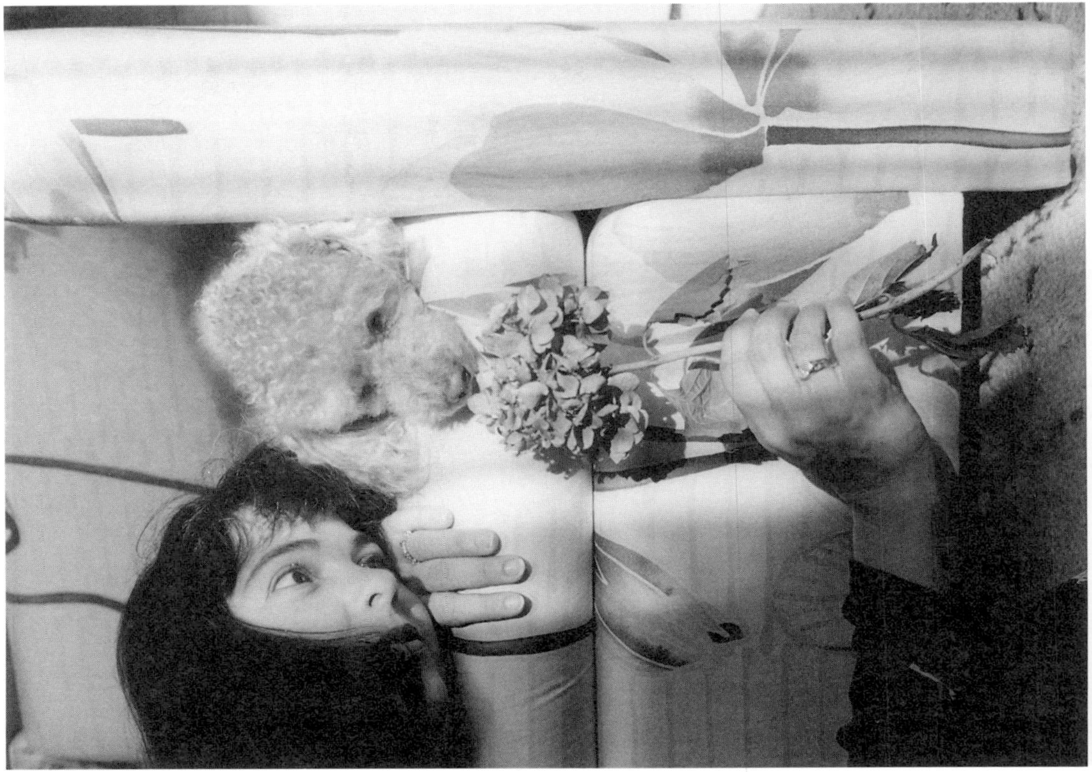

Monday, May 20

*Each one of us is called by God to
be something unique in the universe.
Your life and mine are the unfolding
discovery of what that call means.*

—ALLA RENÉE BOZARTH

Tuesday, May 21

*How aware are you of the gifts
you have received over the course
of your lifetime?*

—JANE MARIE THIBAULT

Wednesday, May 22

_Why should anyone read a
book instead of watching big
people move on a screen?
Because a book can be literature._

—ANNIE DILLARD

Thursday, May 23

_All women have a special ministry,
not only those who become priests
and ministers of the church._

—ANN BELFORD ULANOV

Friday, May 24

The transcendence of God is
in its primary and most important
sense the invisible face of God,
that aspect or dimension that
we never see, never know.

—SALLIE MCFAGUE

Saturday, May 25

The fire is burning in your life;
don't let it go out.

—LAVON BAYLER

Sunday, May 26

ACTS 2:1-21 (NUMBERS 11:24-30)

PSALM 104:24-34, 35B

1 CORINTHIANS 12:3B-13 (ACTS 2:1-21)

JOHN 20:19-23 (JOHN 7:37-39)

There are varieties of working,

but it is the same God who inspires

them all in everyone.

—1 CORINTHIANS 12:7

*I write because there are **stories** that people have forgotten to tell, because I am a woman trying to **stand up** in my life. . . . I am trying to come **alive,** to find the distances in my own recesses and bring them forward and give them color and form.*

—NATALIE GOLDBERG

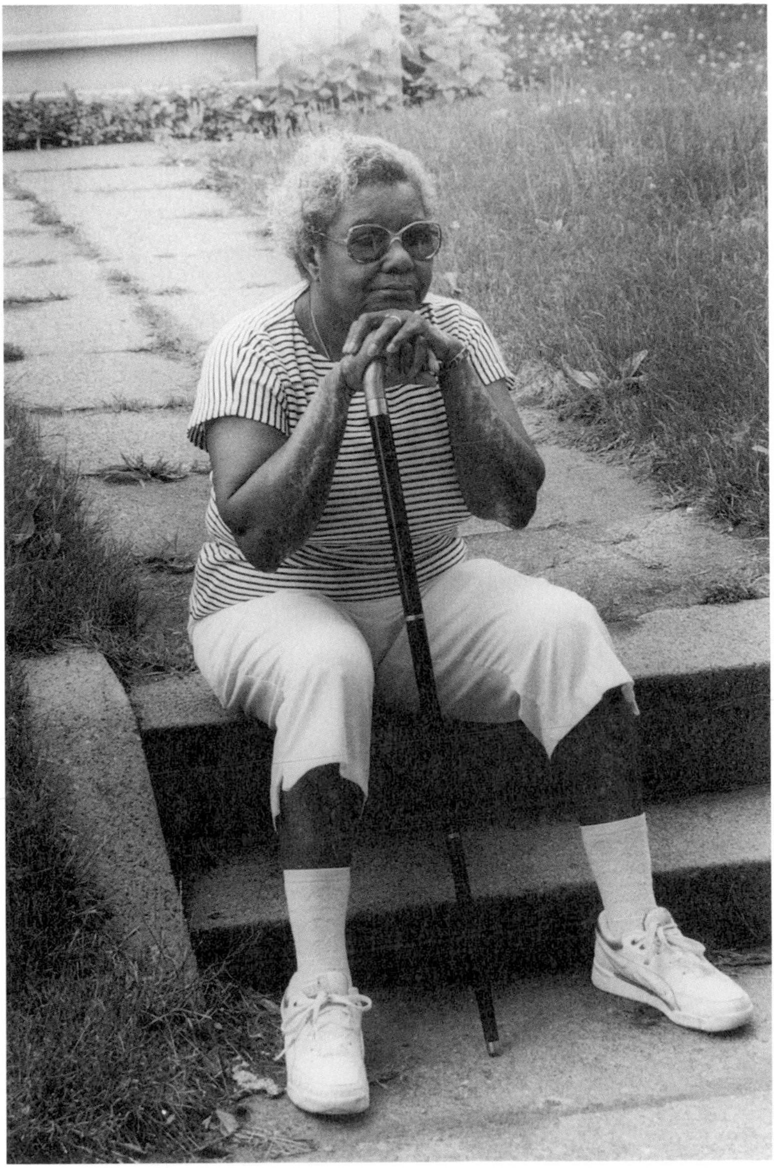

CLEO, *Untitled*, ©1995

Monday, May 27

Sorrow carved into my heart a large
capacity for joy and peace which walk
hand in hand with redemptive love.

—CAROLE F. CHASE

Tuesday, May 28

By their new thoughts and actions
women are saying that they are
***already on their way** toward freedom.*

—LETTY M. RUSSELL

Wednesday, May 29

The journey of holiness is not a
journey with a beginning or an end.
—BETH A. RICHARDSON

Thursday, May 30

I live in a dream world, because
in me the past and the future have
come together.
—MERCY AMBA ODUYOYE

Friday, May 31

Called by the name of women, we
must still create ourselves as women.

—KIM CHERNIN

Saturday, June 1

Should the creation story be
interpreted as placing women
at the top of the hierarchy, created
last . . . as the perfection and
perfectibility of humankind?

—BLU GREENBERG

Sunday, June 2

TRINITY SUNDAY

GENESIS 1:1–2:4A

PSALM 8

2 CORINTHIANS 13:11–13

MATTHEW 28:16–20

So God created humankind in God's image,

in the image of God they were created

male and female God created them.

—GENESIS 1:27

*The truth is, I often like **women**. I like their unconventionality. I like their **subtlety**. I like their **anonymity**.*

—VIRGINIA WOOLF

Monday, June 3

Triumph, not just survival,
is possible for women like me,
ordinary women, everywhere.

—Sonia Johnson

Tuesday, June 4

SHE WHO IS can be spoken as a
robust, appropriate name for God.

—Elizabeth A. Johnson

Wednesday, June 5

God never tires of scooping you up
in times of failure or discouragement
. . . that is God's immense delight!
—JANE MARIE THIBAULT

Thursday, June 6

God is less concerned with efficiency
than faithfulness.
—MARJORY ZOET BANKSON

Friday, June 7

> Every time a woman looks at her
> daughter and thinks, She can be
> anything, she knows in her heart,
> from experience, that it's a lie.
>
> —ANNA QUINDLEN

Saturday, June 8

> I repose in myself. And that part of
> myself, that deepest and richest part in
> which I repose, is what I call "God."
>
> —ETTY HILLESUM

Sunday, June 9

GENESIS 12:1-9/HOSEA 5:15-6:6

PSALM 33:1-2/PSALM 50:7-15

ROMANS 4:13-25

MATTHEW 9:9-13, 18-26

Jesus turned, and seeing her he said, "Take heart, daughter; your faith has made you well."

—MATTHEW 9:22

*This **earth** is my **sister;** I love her daily **grace,** her silent **daring** and how loved I am, **how we admire this strength in each other, all that we have lost, all that we have suffered, all that we know: we are stunned by this beauty,** and I do not forget: what she is to me and what I am to her.*

—SUSAN GRIFFIN

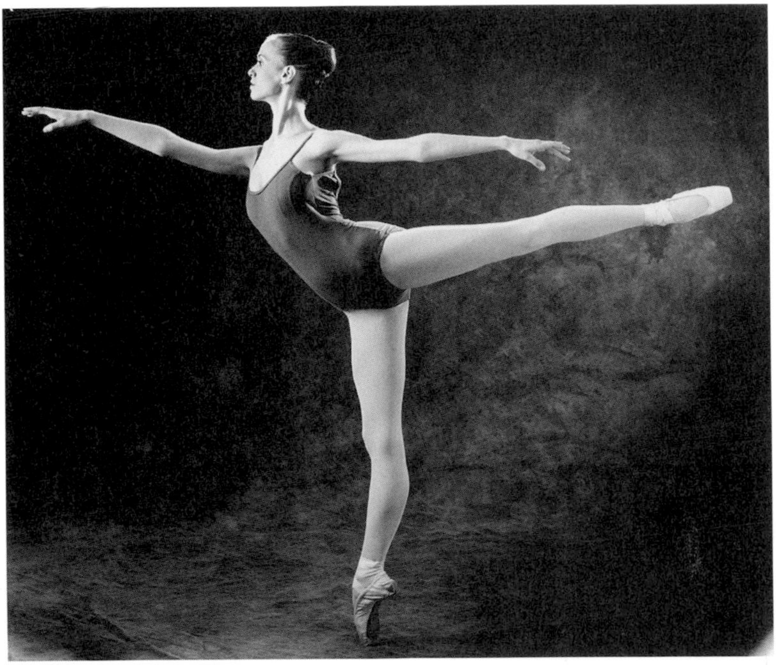

James R. Popovic, Ballerina, ©1994

Monday, June 10

As women begin to establish a
measure of control over the private
areas of their lives through strong
personal decisions, they often gain a
sense of possibilities for acting
effectively in the public realm.

—BARBARA BARKSDALE CLOWSE

Tuesday, June 11

[Ordaining women] acknowledges
that women are made in the
image of God, as men are,
and therefore images for God might
come out of the lives of women.

—LINDA CLARK

Wednesday, June 12

The stories we tell, even the
ones we forget, might be called
the making of sacred text.
—LYNDA SEXSON

Thursday, June 13

The spiritual life does not consist
in mere individual betterment, or
assiduous attention to one's own soul.
—EVELYN UNDERHILL

Friday, June 14

Christian life must always be
the bold attempt to put the words
and belief into practice.

—SALLIE MCFAGUE

Saturday, June 15

[God's love] does not depend upon
our having looked for God first.

—ROBERTA C. BONDI

Sunday, June 16

GENESIS 18:1-15 (21:1-7)/EXODUS 19:2-8A

PSALM 116:1-2, 12-19/PSALM 100

ROMANS 5:1-8

MATTHEW 9:35-10:8 (9-23)

So Sarah laughed to herself,

saying, "After I have grown old,

and my husband is old,

shall I have pleasure?"

—GENESIS 18:12

*Both Christian **feminist** theology and biblical interpretation are in the process of **rediscovering** that the Christian gospel cannot be proclaimed if the **women** disciples and what they have done are **not remembered.***

—ELISABETH SCHÜSSLER FIORENZA

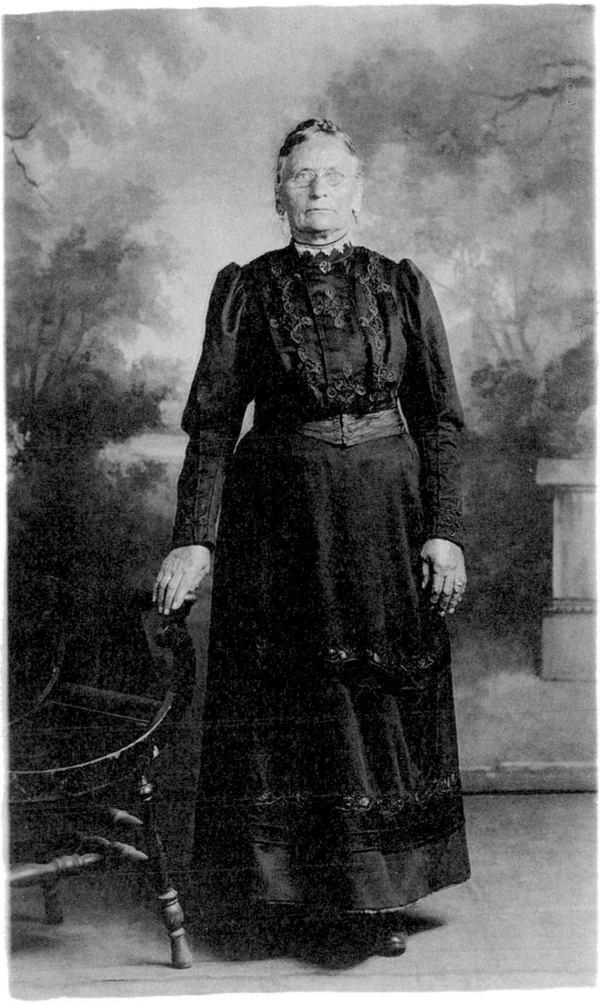

Unknown, Jarosh Family Matriarch, ©1995

Monday, June 17

> *God stays within us as the source of the creative power that moves us both to will and to accomplish.*
>
> —MARIA HARRIS

Tuesday, June 18

> *When suddenly released from conventional relationship structures, we may experience independence as a burden rather than an opportunity.*
>
> —MARJORY ZOET BANKSON

Wednesday, June 19

The stories we tell one another are among our strongest ways of drawing close, of sharing our lives.

—Martha Whitmore Hickman

Thursday, June 20

What have been some of the consequences for women as a result of the traditional understanding of Eve?

—Miriam Therese Winter

Friday, June 21.

> *We empower one another
> by hearing the other to speech.*
> —NELLE MORTON

Saturday, June 22

> *In writing prayers, we struggle with the
> meaning of our relationship with God.*
> —NAOMI JANOWITZ
> AND MAGGIE WENIG

Sunday, June 28

GENESIS 21:8-21/JEREMIAH 20:7-13

PSALM 86:1-10, 16-17/PSALM 69:7-10 (11-15), 16-18

ROMANS 6:1B-11

MATTHEW 10:24-39

Then God opened [Hagar's] eyes

and she saw a well of water. She

went, and filled the skin with water,

and gave the boy a drink.

—GENESIS 21:19

*There is a **spirit** that pervades everything, that is capable of **powerful song** and **radiant movement,** and that moves in and out of the mind. The colors of this spirit are multitudinous, a glowing, pulsing **rainbow.** Old Spider Woman is one name for this quintessential spirit, and Serpent Woman is another. **Corn Woman** is one aspect of her, and Earth Woman is another, and what they together have made is called Creation.*

—PAULA GUNN ALLEN

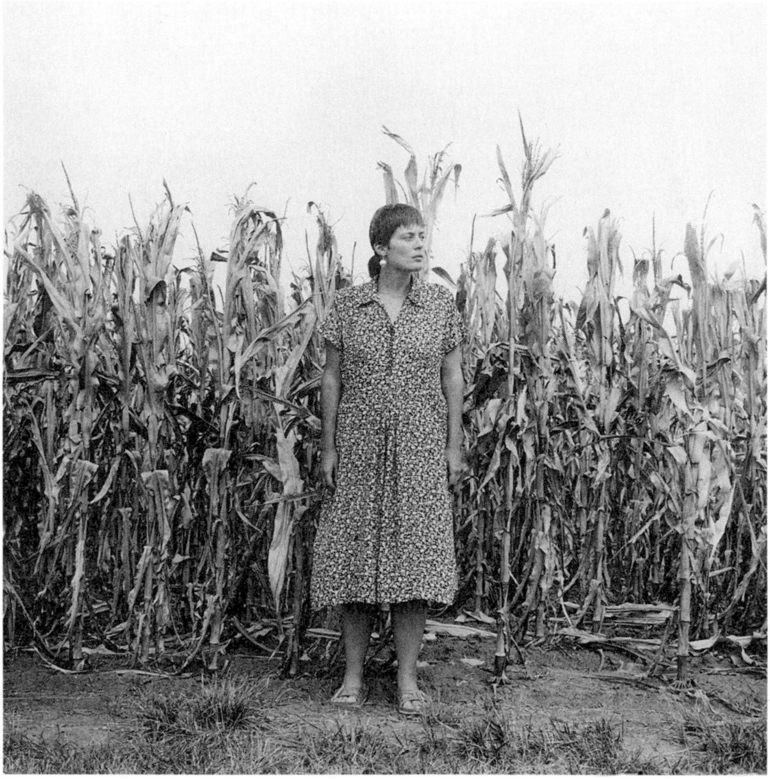

Pat Young, *In Kansas*, ©1988

Monday, June 24

Feminist spirituality proclaims
wholeness, healing love, and spiritual
*power not as hierarchical, as **power over**,*
*but as **power for** as enabling power.*
—ELISABETH SCHÜSSLER FIORENZA

Tuesday, June 25

To be a woman is beautiful
in many more ways than we have
been led to define it.
—PEGGY WAY

Wednesday, June 26

*We always have the choice—to
become bitter with the scars of living,
or to become wounded healers.*

—SALLY PALMER

Thursday, June 27

*The right to criticize comes from a
real relationship, real involvement.*

—LAURA GELLER

Friday, June 28

The Bible is not only a prototype,
it is also a "memory of the future"
that constantly opens up the
possibility of new life.

—LETTY M. RUSSELL

Saturday, June 29

We Marthas can easily fool ourselves
into thinking that we are serving
society, progress, the common good—
or, yes, even ourselves—through our
frantic, fractured, distracted efforts.

—GAIL S. RANSOM

Sunday, June 30

GENESIS 22:1-14/JEREMIAH 28:5-9

PSALM 13/PSALM 89:1-4, 15-18

ROMANS 6:12-23

MATTHEW 10:40-42

And whoever gives to one of these little ones even a cup of cold water because that little one is a disciple, truly, I say to you, the giver shall not go unrewarded.

—MATTHEW 10:42

*The increasing **diversity** of feminist religious discourse calls us to responsibility and to deeper listening, to a commitment to inclusiveness that at the same time allows **individual** and **communal** differences **to emerge.***

—JUDITH PLASKOW AND CAROL P. CHRIST

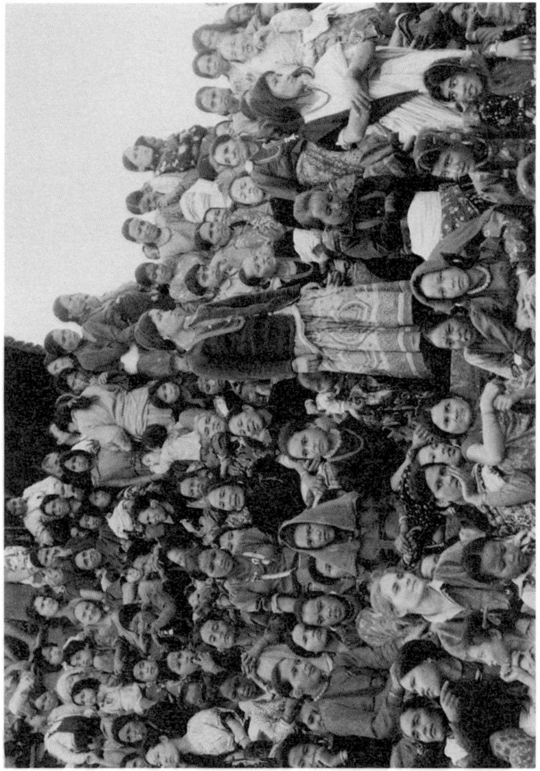

Ian Naysmith, *Indra Jatra,* ©1983

Monday, July 1

CANADA DAY

*Power and authority are given to those
who hear the Word of God and do it, the
disciples. Women can claim this power and
authority to heal their situation.*

—SUSAN BROOKS THISTLETHWAITE

Tuesday, July 2

*Even as feminism announces judgment
on patriarchy and calls for repentance
and change, it needs ever to be
aware of its own potential for idolatry.*

—PHYLLIS TRIBLE

Wednesday, July 3

*Many women of faith . . . believe that
the Bible offers a liberating word for
our times and that the feminist
critical consciousness . . . can unlock
new meaning in scripture.*

—BARBARA BROWN ZIKMUND

Thursday, July 4

INDEPENDENCE DAY

*"Liberty and justice for all" must
include women. Nothing less will do.*

—ANNETTE DAUM

Friday, July 5

Because I see the best of myself in all
humankind, I am buoyed by hope. And
full of faith, especially in women.

—SONIA JOHNSON

Saturday, July 6

I cannot live abundantly without
this community, God's church,
where turning to one another
and working and rejoicing with
one another is a way of life.

—ANN WEEMS

Sunday, July 7

GENESIS 24:34–38, 42–49, 58–67/ZECHARIAH 9:9–12

PSALM 45:10–17 (SONG OF SOLOMON 2:8–13)/PSALM 145:8–14

ROMANS 7:15–25A

MATTHEW 11:16–19, 25–30

Come to me, all who labor and are

heavy laden, and I will give you rest.

—MATTHEW 11:28

*Life is **so rich,** if you can **write** down the real details of the way things **were** and **are,** you hardly need anything else.*

—NATALIE GOLDBERG

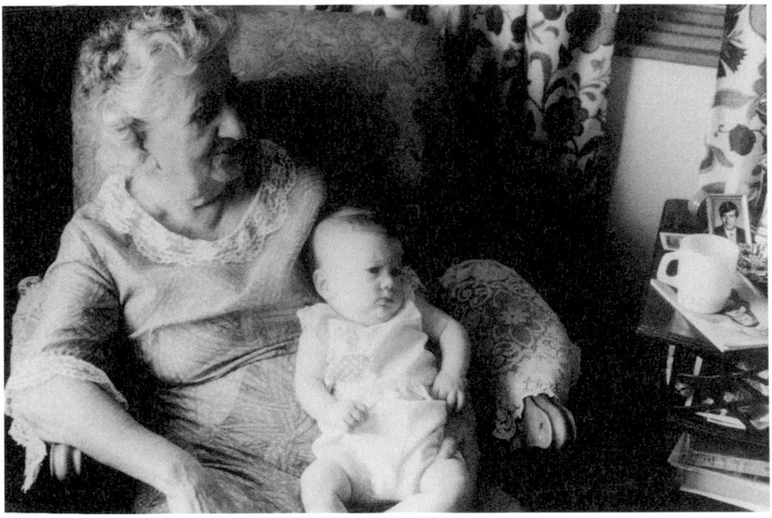

CLEO, Untitled, ©1995

Monday, July 8

When a person understands Justice
the self is let go.

—HILDEGARD OF BINGEN

Tuesday, July 9

I believe we live closer to the truth
of God as we are able to live and
pray comfortably with both masculine
and feminine images of God.

—VIRGINIA ANN FROEHLE

Wednesday, July 10

Listening for God's voice, getting
to our feet, and comforting one
another are often unimaginable acts
in the desert places of our lives.
—MARY ZIMMER

Thursday, July 11

For women, cooperation is both
something we value and something
we recognize to be quite necessary
for our survival.
—CHRISTINE M. SMITH

Friday, July 12

Women's experience, like all human experience, is a source of insight about the divine.

—CAROL P. CHRIST

Saturday, July 13

Forgiveness is giving up the right to retaliate.

—PIXIE KOESTLINE HAMMOND

Sunday, July 14

GENESIS 25:19–34/ISAIAH 55:10–13

PSALM 119:105–112/PSALM 65:(1–8) 9–13

ROMANS 8:1–11

MATTHEW 13:1–9, 18–23

So shall my word be that goes forth from my mouth;

it shall not return to me empty,

but it shall accomplish that which I purpose

and prosper in the thing for which I sent it.

—ISAIAH 55:11

*Every possible **vision** of the female is offered as a **credible option,** leaving us with the intoxicating **freedom** to find our own ways to be women, putting together as best we can a personal combination of background, tradition, innovation, and original experience to **create** a personal **identity** that will hold **authority** for us.*

—ANN BELFORD ULANOV

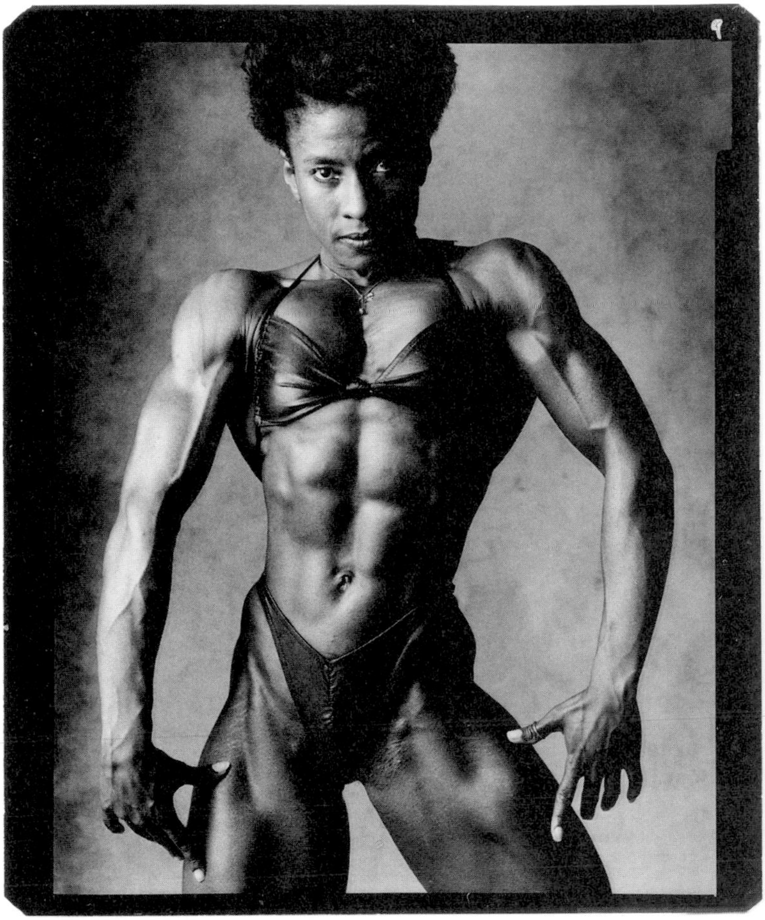

Geoffrey Pankhurst, Sharon, ©1995

Monday, July 15

*By virtue of our being
women we share a common pain.*

—NELLE MORTON

Tuesday, July 16

*Women need to be more
articulate in defining themselves
and their faith experience.*

—MARIE ASSAAD

Wednesday, July 17

A little peace, a lot of kindness and a little wisdom—whenever I have these inside me I feel I am doing well.

—ETTY HILLESUM

Thursday, July 18

[Feminist theology] is in fact about another way of thinking of transcendence.

—DOROTHEE SÖLLE

Friday, July 19

However long her span of years, no woman could outlive her potential for spiritual growth. It exists at any age.

—BARBARA BARKSDALE CLOWSE

Saturday, July 20

Women who have discovered their true selves relate to men as their equals and expect men to do the same.

—CARROLL SAUSSY

Sunday, July 21

GENESIS 28:10–19A/ISAIAH 44:6–8

PSALM 139:1–12, 23–24/PSALM 86:11–17

ROMANS 8:12–25

MATTHEW 13:24–30, 36–43

If I take the wings of the morning

   and dwell in the uttermost parts of the sea,

even there your hand shall lead me,

   and your right hand shall hold me.

—PSALM 139:9–10

*Being **solitary** is being alone well: being alone **luxuriously**
immersed in doings of your own **choice,** aware of the fullness
of your **own presence** rather than of the absence of others.*

—ALICE KOLLER

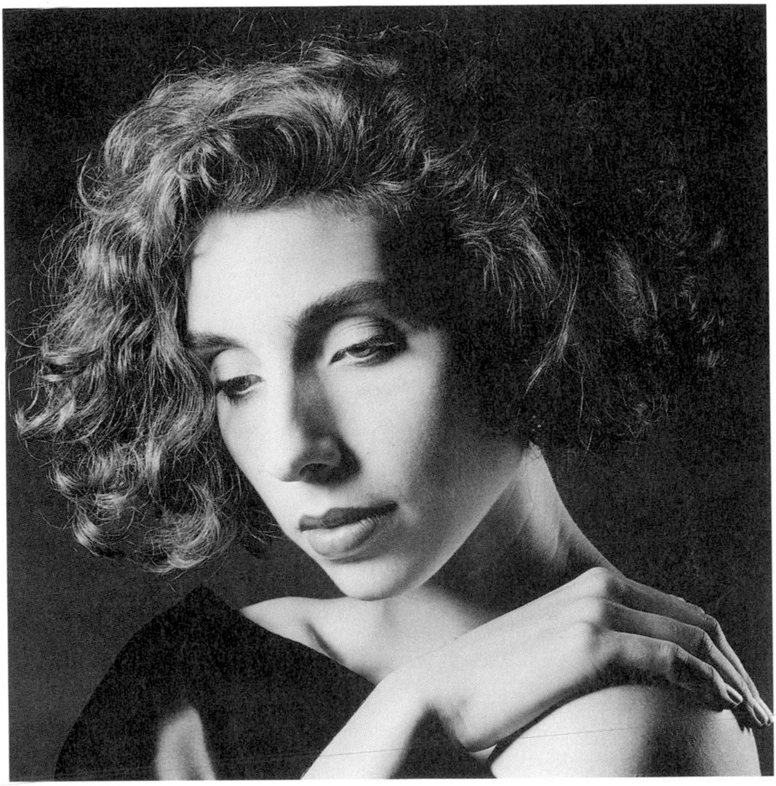

Jesse L. Kramer, *Untitled*, ©1990

Monday, July 22

*We are a domesticated species
and we need to take back the
wildness that is in us.*

—KIM CHERNIN

Tuesday, July 23

*To help women to earn their
livings in the professions is to help
them to possess that weapon of
independent opinion which is still
their most powerful weapon.*

—VIRGINIA WOOLF

Wednesday, July 24

A feminist moral theology celebrates the

power of our human praxis as an

*intrinsic aspect of the work of **God's** love.*

—BEVERLY WILDUNG HARRISON

Thursday, July 25

The most fundamental or transformative

events can come in the smallest images.

—LYNDA SEXSON

Friday, July 26

*Knead us together into one loaf
with all your people throughout the
world, through your Spirit of unity.*

—Ruth C. Duck

Saturday, July 27

*It is never easy to demand
the most from ourselves,
from our lives, from our work.*

—Audre Lord

Sunday, July 28

GENESIS 29:15-28/1 KINGS 3:5-12

PSALM 105:1-11, 45B (PSALM 128)/PSALM 119:129-136

ROMANS 8:26-39

MATTHEW 13:31-33, 44-52

We know that in everything

God works for good with those

who love God, who are called

according to God's purpose.

—ROMANS 8:28

*To **face depression** and **seek healing** is an act of the heart, an en-Spirited heart that knows an **intimate** way to its own **healing.** For when we live most deeply in our own hearts, we also live in the very heart of God.*

—JEAN M. BLOMQUIST

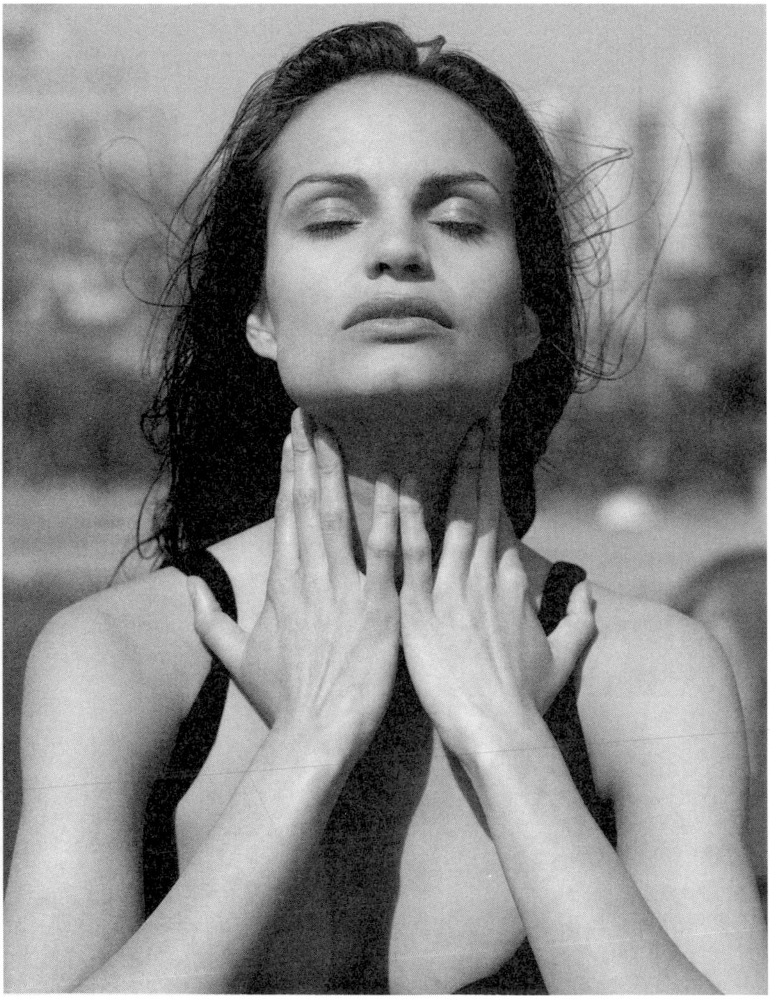

Donald Lesko, *Untitled*, ©1994

Monday, July 29

*Before you can know whether
what you say is true, you must first
know what you mean to say.*

—ALICE KOLLER

Tuesday, July 30

*As a critique of culture and
faith in light of misogyny, feminism
is a prophetic movement.*

—PHYLLIS TRIBLE

Wednesday, July 31

As ***imago Dei*** *[weeping women]*
point to the mystery of divine
sorrow, of an unimaginable
compassionate God who suffers
with beloved creation.
—ELIZABETH A. JOHNSON

Thursday, August 1

It is in our cooperation with a
God who is love and who acts in
history through us, that we may
find the peace that the Spirit, in
Her Wisdom, has made available to
us from the beginning.
—CARTER HEYWARD

Friday, August 2

The gift of forgiveness will always feel incomplete if it does not bear fruit in reconciliation.

—MARJORIE J. THOMPSON

Saturday, August 3

A pedestal is as much a prison as any other small space.

—ANONYMOUS

Sunday, August 4

GENESIS 32:22-31/ISAIAH 55:1-5

PSALM 17:1-7, 15/PSALM 145:8-9, 14-21

ROMANS 9:1-5

MATTHEW 14:13-21

I call upon you, for you will answer me, O God;

incline your ear to me, hear my words.

—PSALM 17:6

*I began to think of the **soul** as if it were a **castle** made of a single diamond or of very clear **crystal,** in which there are many **rooms.***

—St. Teresa of Avila

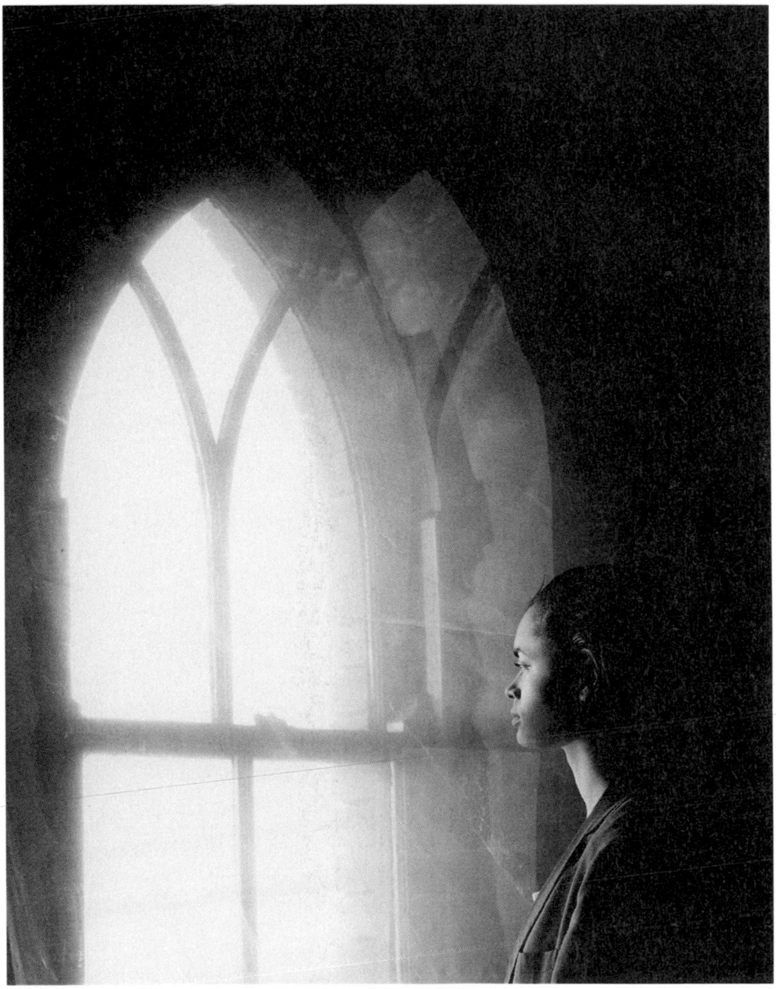

Geoffrey Pankhurst, Tara, ©1995

Monday, August 5

The world is our meeting place with God.

—SALLIE McFAGUE

Tuesday, August 6

Try to learn tranquillity, to live in the
present a part of the time every day.

—BRENDA UELAND

Wednesday, August 7

_____
_____
_____
_____
_____
_____
_____
_____
_____
_____
_____

*One of the myths of our culture
is that control of ourselves and
others is what gives us freedom.*
—JUDITH E. SMITH

Thursday, August 8

_____
_____
_____
_____
_____
_____
_____

*Given the opportunity to confront
our own pain and prejudice, to
challenge our own assumptions, to
tell and retell our own stories, we are
encouraged and empowered through
collective wisdom shared.*
—MIRIAM THERESE WINTER

Friday, August 9

---

*In hearing and naming ourselves out of the depths, women are naming **toward** God, which is what theology always should have been about.*

—MARY DALY

Saturday, August 10

To speak of God is among the most difficult and audacious things that humans do.

—RITA M. GROSS

Sunday, August 11

GENESIS 37:1-4, 12-28/1 KINGS 19:9-18

PSALM 105: 1-6, 16-22, 45B/PSALM 85:8-13

ROMANS 10:5-15

MATTHEW 14:22-33

For if it is believed with the heart, there is righteousness, and if it is confessed with the mouth there is salvation.

—ROMANS 10:10

Discovering my true *identity* didn't take place in one great big dramatic moment. It was a *slow* and sometimes *painful process.*

—ROSE MARY DENMAN

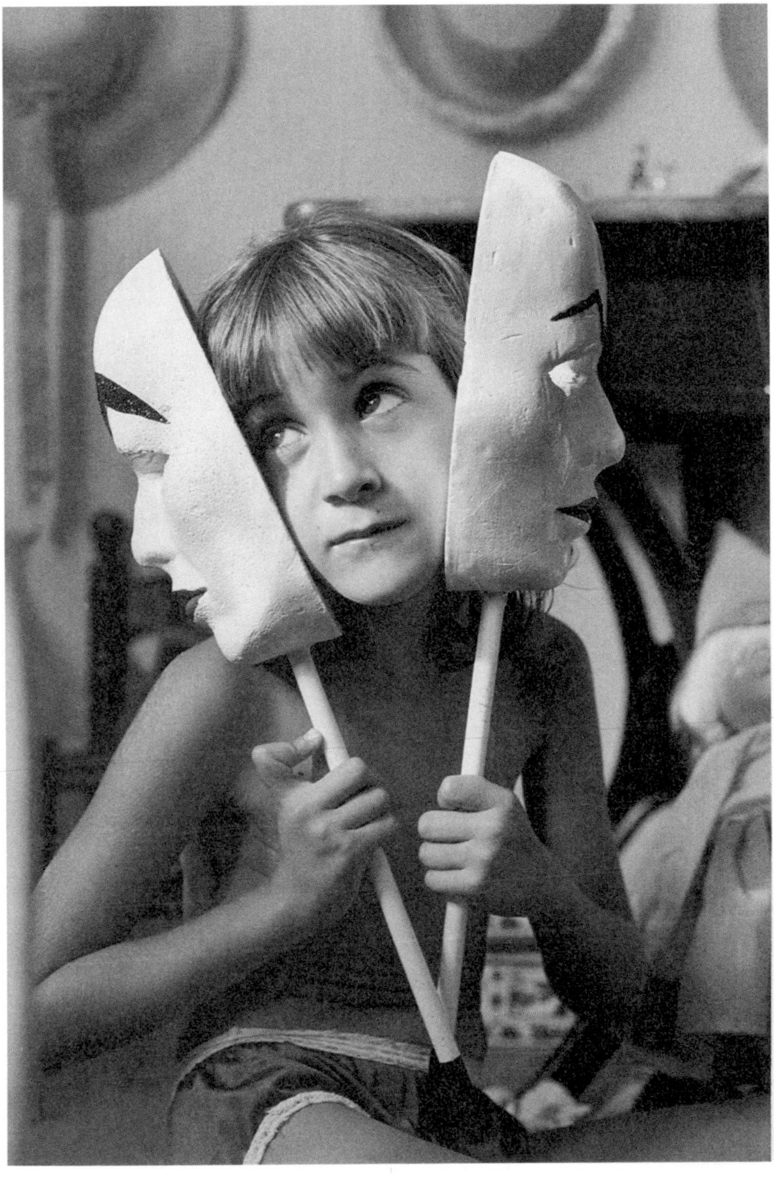

Marilyn C. Szalay, *Mary Jane in the Fantasy Room,* ©1982

Monday, August 12

> *The diversity within feminist theology and spirituality is its strength.*
>
> —CAROL P. CHRIST
> AND JUDITH PLASKOW

Tuesday, August 13

> *We must **daily** struggle with decisions and with self, refusing to let go of God.*
>
> —CAROLE A. RAYBURN

Wednesday, August 14

When clergy and laity engage in
ministry together, the whole people
of God bear responsibility for
decision-making.
—ROSEMARY KELLER

Thursday, August 15

We were created in God's own
being, to move with God, in God,
by God, into the passion and the
pain and the wonder of creation.
—CARTER HEYWARD

Friday, August 16

> *In prayer we cry to God for help.*
> *But do we know what we want?*
> —MARGARET W. CROCKETT-CANNON

Saturday, August 17

> *Our greatness lies in our concern*
> *for the lost ones in our midst.*
> —CAROLE CARLSON

Sunday, August 18

GENESIS 45:1–15/ISAIAH 56:1, 6–8

PSALM 133/PSALM 67

ROMANS 11:1–2A, 29–32

MATTHEW 15:(10–20) 21–28

And a Canaanite woman from that region came out and cried, "Have mercy on me, Sovereign, Son of David, my daughter is severely possessed by a demon."

—MATTHEW 15:22

*We forget that we too are **children** whose hearts must be **opened, trusting** and **needful** of God's deep embrace where all joy, all suffering is felt and borne.*

—WENDY M. WRIGHT

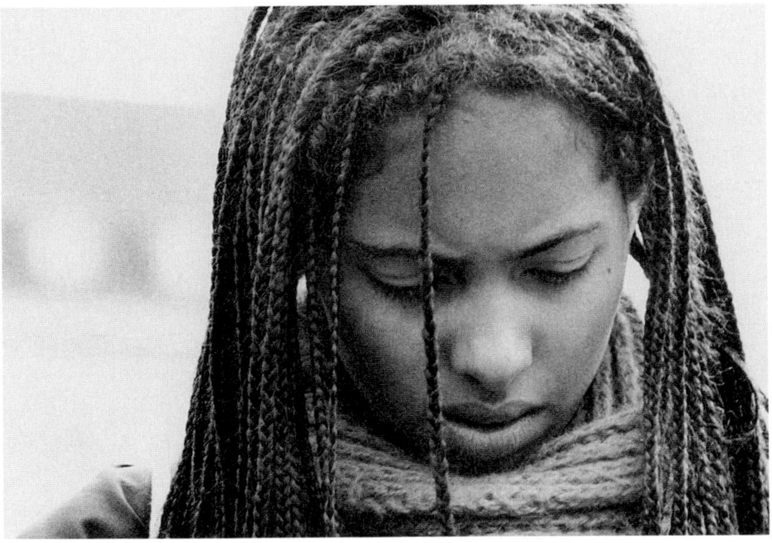

Luke Golobitsh, *Teen at Bonn, Germany, Demo,* ©1994

Monday, August 19

*In ever-new images and symbols,
feminist liturgies seek to rename the
God of the Bible and the biblical vision.*
—ELISABETH SCHÜSSLER FIORENZA

Tuesday, August 20

*Our yeasty richness will
leaven and change the world.*
—SONIA JOHNSON

Wednesday, August 21

The uniqueness of feminist theology
is not the critical principle of "full
humanity" but that women claim this
principle for themselves.
—ROSEMARY RADFORD RUETHER

Thursday, August 22

It might be useful to figure out
precisely when I got hooked on not
competing with women.
—LETTY COTTIN POGREBIN

Friday, August 23

Holy persons draw to themselves
all that is earthly.
—HILDEGARD OF BINGEN

Saturday, August 24

We seek those qualities,
those images of God for which
we have the greatest need at any
one time of our lives.
—VIRGINIA ANN FROEHLE

Sunday, August 25

EXODUS 1:8–2:10/ISAIAH 51:1–6

PSALM 124/PSALM 138

ROMANS 12:1–8

MATTHEW 16:13–20

But the midwives feared God,

and did not do as the king of

Egypt commanded them,

but let the male children live.

—EXODUS 1:17

---

*God is **intimately aware** of our thoughts before we **utter**
them, of our **hidden** motives, of our most **secret** emotions.*

—CATHERINE GUNSALUS GONZÁLEZ

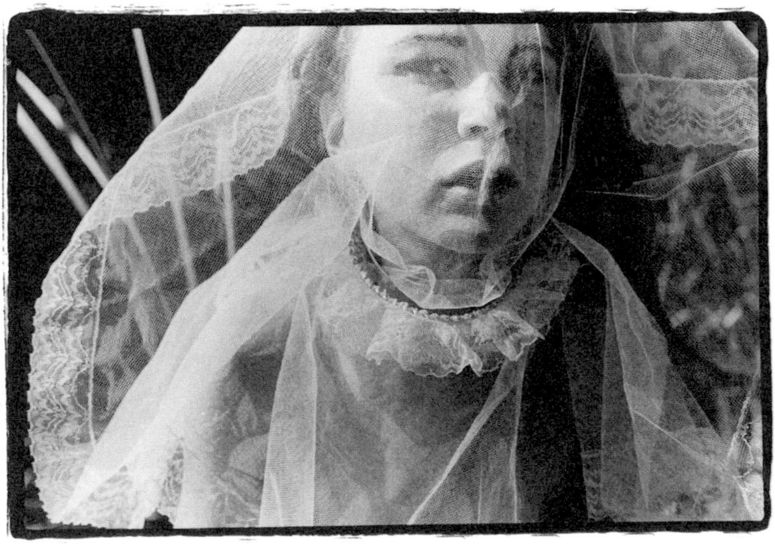

Marilyn C. Szalay, *Lost Madonna*, ©1984

Monday, August 26

Our theologizing as women
is part of a vast continuum that
includes the sacred energies
of the hidden women of history.
—ALLA RENÉE BOZARTH

Tuesday, August 27

Clinging to the past is the problem.
Embracing change is the solution.
—GLORIA STEINEM

Wednesday, August 28

One of the tasks of discipleship is
to distinguish truth from untruth.
—WENDY MILLER

Thursday, August 29

Identifying and describing any
person in the pulpit or classroom by
their sex function is immoral.
—NELLE MORTON

Friday, August 30

May God keep you safe until the word of your life is fully spoken.

—MARGARET FULLER

Saturday, August 31

By becoming whole persons, women can generate a counterforce to the stereotype of the leader as they challenge the artificial polarization of human characteristics.

—MARY DALY

Sunday, September 1

EXODUS 3:1-15/JEREMIAH 15:15-21

PSALM 105: 1-6, 23-26, 45c/PSALM 26:1-8

ROMANS 12:9-21

MATTHEW 16:21-28

Rejoice in your hope, be patient in

tribulation, be constant in prayer.

Contribute to the needs of the

saints, practice hospitality.

—ROMANS 12:12–13

*Our **culture** may find itself alienated from its textual tra-dition, but **human beings** are never "textless"—we cannot help making text, formulating our **images** into **phrases,** our **dreams** into **lives.***

—LYNDA SEXSON

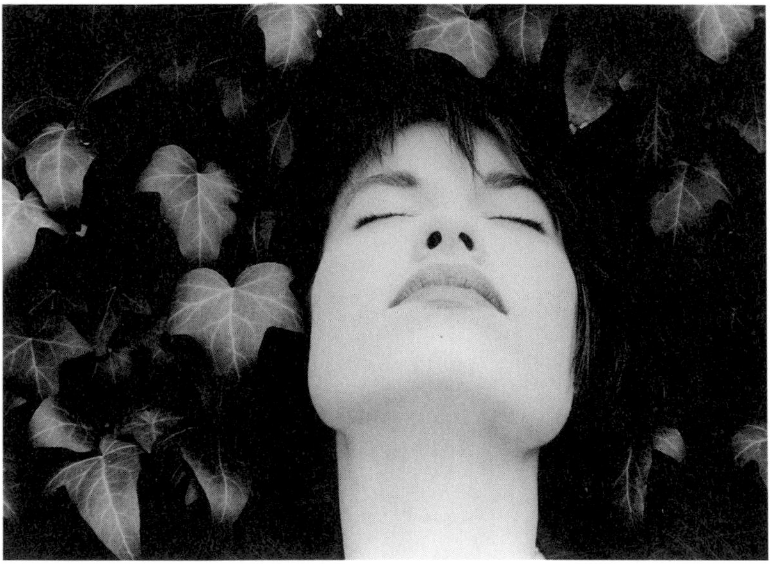

Vaccariello, *Penny in Ivy,* ©1991

Monday, September 2

LABOR DAY

The striking amount of biblical
material that recounts Jesus' special
regard for women . . . was the beginning
point for the development of a feminist
interpretation of the Bible.
—SUSAN BROOKS THISTLETHWAITE

Tuesday, September 3

The God-images we inherit
and those we choose to use in
prayer shape our lives.
—VIRGINIA ANN FROEHLE

Wednesday, September 4

A healthy, ascetic discipline asks you
to rejoice in these gifts of deprivation,
to learn from them and to care less
for amenities than for that which
refreshes from a deeper source.

—KATHLEEN NORRIS

Thursday, September 5

[The Gentile woman's] gift was also
the gift of courage—the courage of
those who have little more to lose
and therefore can act in commitment
and from faith on behalf of others.

—SHARON H. RINGE

Friday, September 6

_____
_____
_____
_____
_____
_____
_____
_____
_____

The task of feminist hermeneutics is

. . . to see to it that the memory of

this interpretation will not again be

erased from the collective memory of

the communities of biblical faith.

—ROSEMARY RADFORD RUETHER

Saturday, September 7

_____
_____
_____
_____
_____
_____
_____
_____

As believer, the teacher is part

of a community that lives in

response to God's claim upon it,

teaching of God's grace.

—HULDA NIEBUHR

Sunday, September 8

EXODUS 12:1-14/EZEKIEL 33:7-11

PSALM 149/PSALM 119:33-40

ROMANS 13:8-14

MATTHEW 18:15-20

For where two or three are gathered in my name, there I am in the midst of them.

—MATTHEW 18:20

*I try to live in fidelity toward the **twin vision** of **friendship** and **justice**—of a time when the structures of enemyhood will be broken, when **people** and the **earth** can move toward patterns of healing and health . . . when the artistry of **each life** will be **valued** above rubies.*

—ELEANOR H. HANEY

Geoffrey Pankhurst, *The Morris Twins*, ©1990

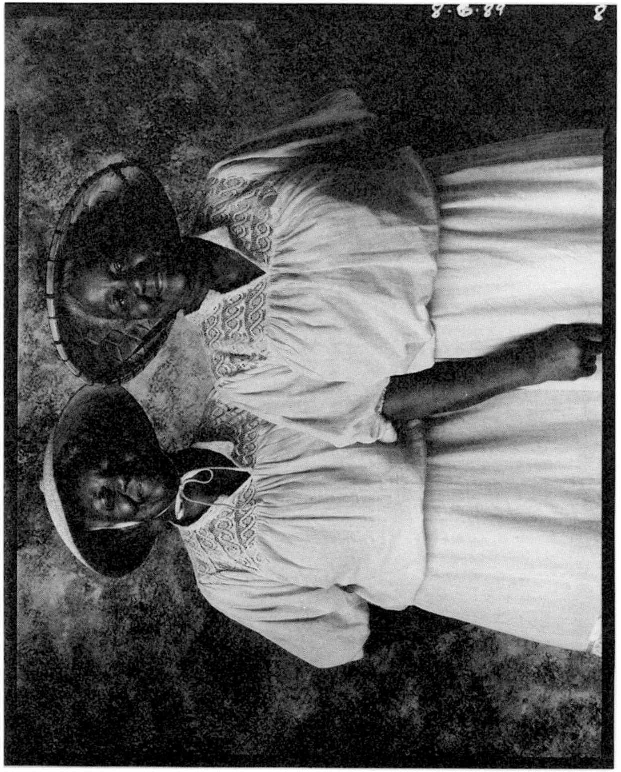

Monday, September 9

Feminist theology . . . is fascinating
*for women because **women** are*
reflecting their situation.
—ELISABETH MOLTMANN-WENDEL

Tuesday, September 10

I believe that only in the union
of justice with suffering love
is any human force redemptive
and permanently curative.
—GEORGIA HARKNESS

Wednesday, September 11

It is possible that a feminist
hermeneutic can allow more scales to
drop from our eyes, so that the biblical
witness is freed for our seeing.
—MARGARET A. FARLEY

Thursday, September 12

Art requires a delicate adjustment
of the outer and inner worlds in
such a way that, without changing
their nature, they can be seen
through each other.
—FLANNERY O'CONNOR

Friday, September 13

One of the cardinal principles of good
interreligious dialogue: people deal in
their own first-hand experience.

—VIRGINIA RAMEY MOLLENKOTT

Saturday, September 14

ROSH HASHANAH

Women do more than raise the
question. We are the question.

—NELLE MORTON

Sunday, September 15

Exodus 14:19-31/Genesis 50:15-21

Psalm 114 (Exodus 15:1b-11, 20-21)/Psalm 103 (1-7) 8-13

Romans 14:1-12

Matthew 18:21-35

And Miriam sang to them:

"Sing to God, who has triumphed gloriously;

horse and rider God has thrown into the sea."

—Exodus 15:21

*With my **sisters,** I seek **mirrors** for the creation of a theal-ogy that would empower our struggles with racism, sexism, economic exploitation, and narrow nationalism. In the search to create a thealogy that affirms our lives, we seek **divine images** and a **spiritual depth** that connect us to all our worlds. . . . We seek a thealogy that **binds our worlds** in a life-giving wisdom.*

—RITA NAKASHIMA BROCK

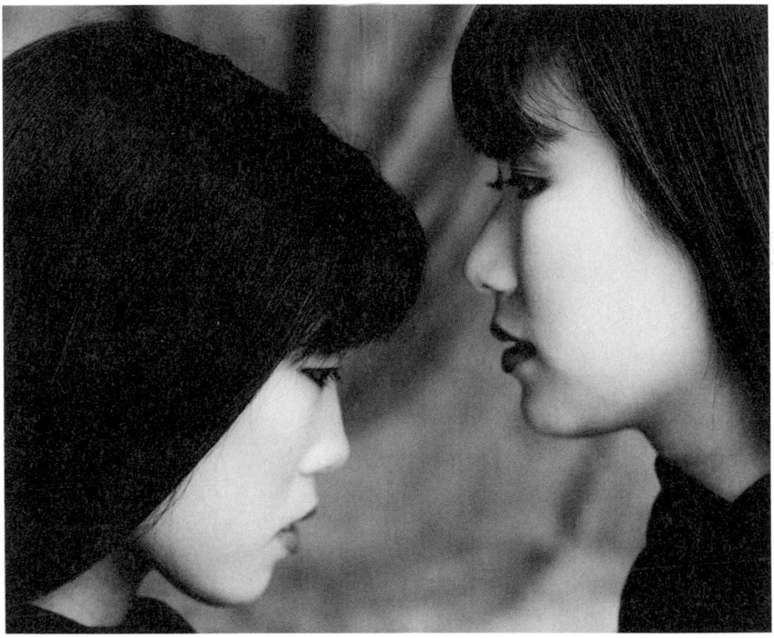

Vaccariello, *Sisters*, ©1971

Monday, September 16

*The whole of creation is on
tiptoe to see the wonderful sight
of the daughters and sons of God
coming into their own.*
—MARY SUE GAST

Tuesday, September 17

*Women may well ask: . . . What
helps to link us to the great women
of our tradition?*
—KATHLEEN HUGHES

Wednesday, September 18

The prodigal daughter of God is the one
who returns to herself, to the fatherly
arms of God who is our mother.
—ELISABETH MOLTMANN-WENDEL

Thursday, September 19

Grant us the courage of Ruth to
leave behind the old and familiar.
—MARILEE SCROGGS

Friday, September 20

Virginia Woolf changed my life;
the melodramatic hint of
conversion seems appropriate.

—SARA RUDDICK

Saturday, September 21

Philippians . . . and Acts . . .
indicate that women played important
roles in founding the community
and in its preaching mission.

—PHEME PERKINS

Sunday, September 22

Only let your manner of life be

worthy of the gospel of Christ.

—PHILIPPIANS 1:27

*You are **called** quietly and constantly to **stretch beyond** the comfortable to reach for your own freedom and to help others do the same. But because there is always so much to **distract** you from yourself in the everyday, **external world,** God will constantly draw you within your soul and will speak to your **heart.***

—JANE MARIE THIBAULT

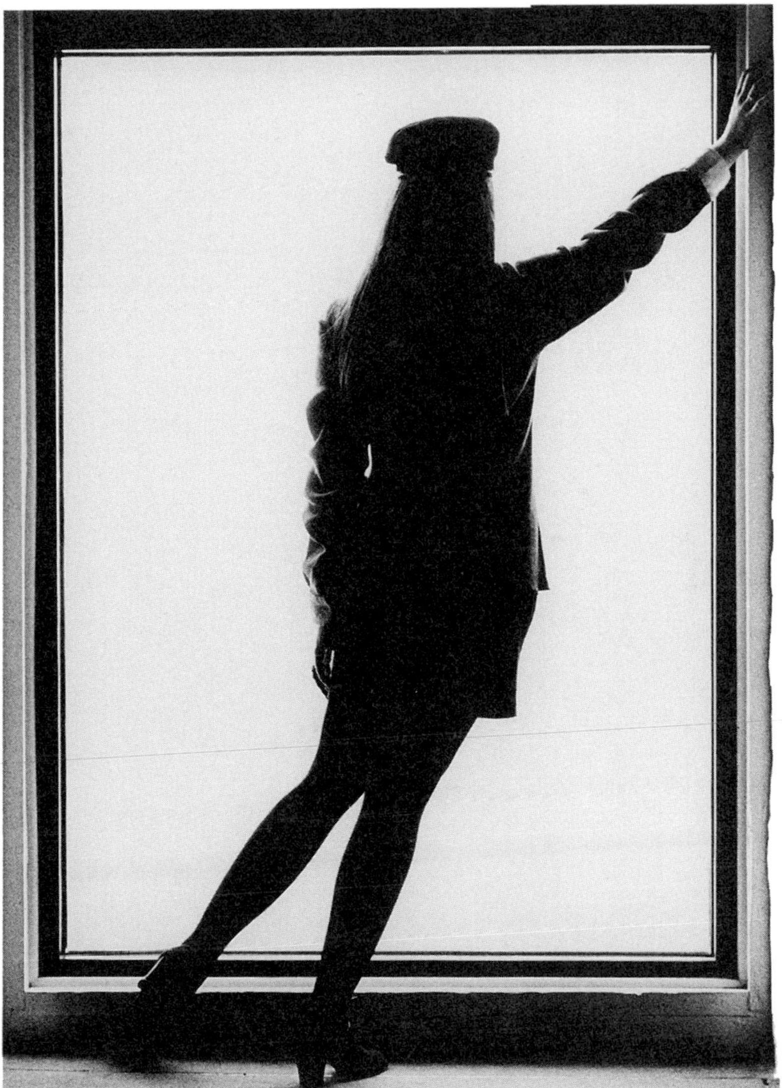

Jesse L. Kramer, Untitled, ©1994

Monday, September 23

YOM KIPPUR

*In the different voice of women
lies the truth of an ethic of care.*

—CAROL GILLIGAN

Tuesday, September 24

*Just as we were to be without
end, so we were treasured and
hidden in God, known and loved
from without beginning.*

—JULIAN OF NORWICH

Wednesday, September 25

Women and women's work . . .
will never be taken seriously
unless women take it seriously.
—LINDA ELLERBEE

Thursday, September 26

Work without neglect to promote
Love above all things.
—HADEWIJCH

Friday, September 27

_____
_____
_____
_____
_____
_____
_____
_____

> We need to uncover and (re)write our
> own multistoried history, and to talk
> to one another as we are doing so.
>
> —GLORIA T. HULL

Saturday, September 28

_____
_____
_____
_____
_____
_____
_____
_____

> Women have . . . claimed the
> psalms as their own by singing
> "new songs."
>
> —KATHLEEN A. FARMER

Sunday, September 29

Lead me in your truth, and teach me,

for you are the God of my salvation.

—PSALM 25:5

I have come to believe that **prayer** *is not a matter of* my

calling in an attempt to get God's attention, but of my

finally listening to the call of God, *which has been con-*

stant, patient, and insistent in my **inner being.**

—VIRGINIA RAMEY MOLLENKOTT

Vaccariello, *Untitled*, ©1992

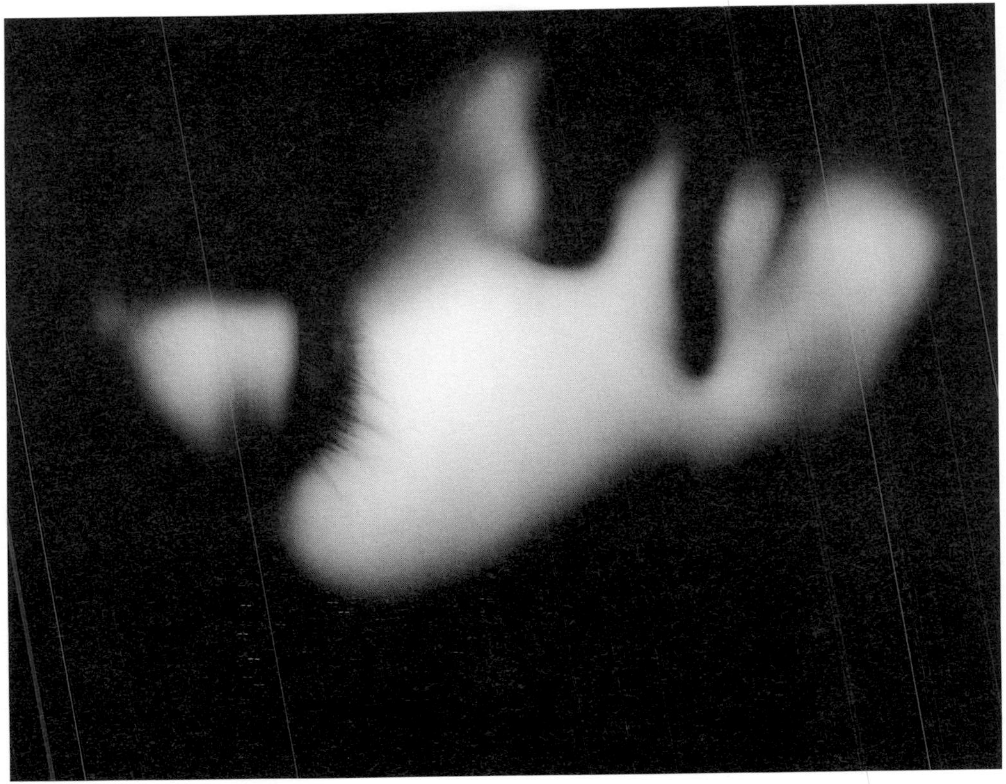

Monday, September 30

It's a very loving experience for me to photograph someone. I care about people in a different way once I've photographed them.

—LYNDA KOOLISH

Tuesday, October 1

O God, in mystery and silence you are present in our lives.

—RUTH C. DUCK

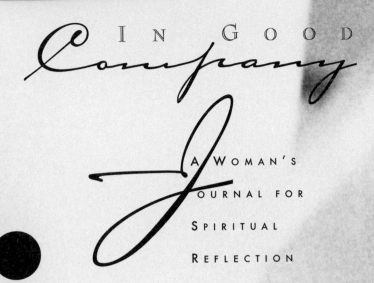

IN GOOD Company

A WOMAN'S JOURNAL FOR SPIRITUAL REFLECTION

s now available at your local bookstore . . .

- more beautiful photography
- fresh and insightful quotations
- unique journal format for your own reflections
- weekly selections from the *Revised Common Lectionary*
- complete bibliography for further reading

A wonderful gift for yourself or for women you know for whom spiritual reflection is an important part of their daily lives.

Contact your local bookstore or call 1-800-537-3394 for information on how you can order the 1997 edition of **In Good Company.**

1 9 9 7

A Call for Quotes

n your reading during the past year, have you come across any quotes you would like to submit for future editions of **In Good Company?** *If so, now is the time to send them in. If we use your submission, we will include your name in the acknowledgments.*

When submitting quotes, please be sure that the selections are brief (1–2 sentences) and taken only from prose sources (no poetry or music). Include a photocopy of the page from which the quote is taken, along with a copy of the title page and copyright page of the book. Send your submissions to:

IN GOOD COMPANY
The Pilgrim Press
700 Prospect Avenue East
Cleveland OH 44115-1100

Wednesday, October 2

It is possible to be a solitary in one's mind while living in a crowd, and it is possible for one who is a solitary to live in the crowd of one's own thoughts.

—DESERT MOTHER SYNCLETICA

Thursday, October 3

I insist upon spending this time to the best advantage. I will go down with my colors flying.

—VIRGINIA WOOLF

Friday, October 4

The stronger our identity, the more we
cultivate a deeper knowledge of our past.
—KATHLEEN HUGHES

Saturday, October 5

The message of our sister Huldah [the
prophet] is "Speak up. Write letters.
Share your insights and wisdom."
—MARY ZIMMER

Sunday, October 6

EXODUS 20:1-4, 7-9, 12-20/ISAIAH 5:1-7

PSALM 19/PSALM 80:7-15

PHILIPPIANS 3:4B-14

MATTHEW 21:33-46

But who can discern one's errors?

Cleanse me from hidden faults.

—PSALM 19:12

Womanist theological *vision* will grow as [African American] women come together and **connect** piece with piece. Between the process of creating and the sense of calling, womanist theology will one day present itself in full array, **reflecting** the divine spirit that connects us all.

—DELORES S. WILLIAMS

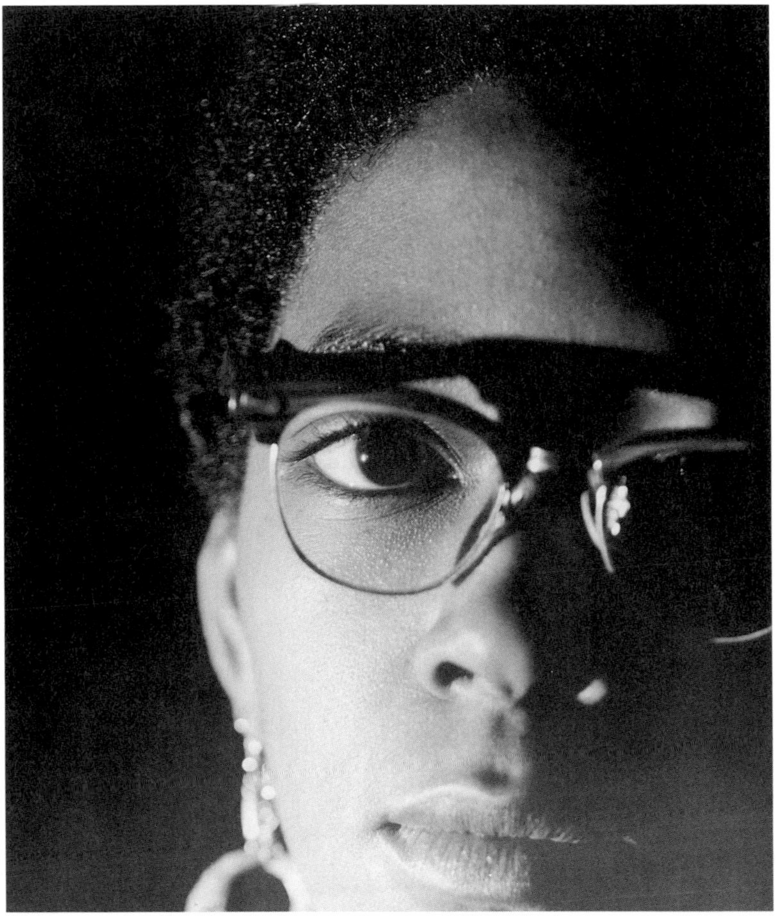

Amy Sorokas, *Untitled*, ©1994

Monday, October 7

*The more sensitive we become to
history, the more conscious we are
of our present identity and our
future possibilities.*

—KATHLEEN HUGHES

Tuesday, October 8

*Our endless friendship, our place,
our life and our being are in God.*

—JULIAN OF NORWICH

Wednesday, October 9

The images of God in the Bible . . .
were and are open for theophantasy.
—ELISABETH MOLTMANN-WENDEL

Thursday, October 10

Being a feminist means giving back
better than we got, when it comes to
respect, and it means respecting the
work—and the choices—of women.
—LINDA ELLERBEE

Friday, October 11

> The two major contributions of
> every lesbian and gay person who is
> out are love and honesty.
> —MARY E. HUNT

Saturday, October 12

> For women in particular, the
> passage from ancient text to
> contemporary context is . . .
> dynamic and multidimensional.
> —SHARON H. RINGE

Sunday, October 18

EXODUS 32:1-14/ISAIAH 25:1-9

PSALM 106:1-6, 19-23/PSALM 23

PHILIPPIANS 4:1-9

MATTHEW 22:1-14

And the peace of God, which passes

all understanding, will keep your

hearts and your minds in Christ Jesus.

—PHILIPPIANS 4:7

*It is one of the **encouraging** recognitions of feminist theology that at the passion of Jesus there were **women** who remained with him after all the men had run off. They **stood under** the cross from **afar**. . . . Today, too, women stand under the cross.*

—DOROTHEE SÖLLE

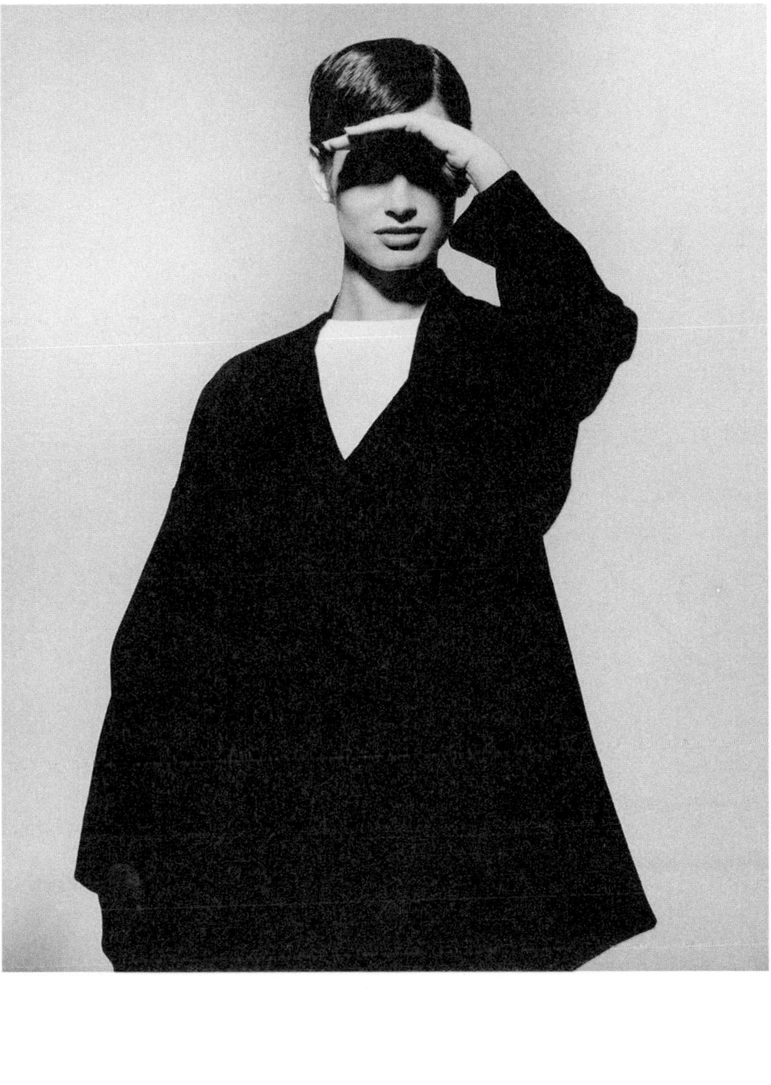

Vaccariello, *Untitled*, ©1994

Monday, October 14

THANKSGIVING DAY (CANADA)

*Among the most pressing items on the agenda for research on adult development is the need to delineate **in women's own terms** the experience of their adult life.*

—CAROL GILLIGAN

Tuesday, October 15

There is a symbolic science that surrounds [African American] women's public identities.

—ERLENE STETSON

Wednesday, October 16

When the psalms are sung by
women's voices . . . then the God
whom our ancestors called "the God
of Jacob" becomes the refuge and
the strength of women.

—KATHLEEN A. FARMER

Thursday, October 17

To be in touch with our passion and to
acknowledge our passion as a gift of
God's "good" Creation is to give birth
to a new way of being in the world.

—PATRICIA L. HUNTER

Friday, October 18

> *Being a woman is hard work.*
> *Not without joy and even ecstasy,*
> *but still relentless, unending work.*
>
> —MAYA ANGELOU

Saturday, October 19

> *A feminist approach to understanding*
> *biblical materials . . . evaluates the*
> *authority of texts on the basis of their*
> *affirmation of the full humanity of women.*
>
> —DRORAH O'DONNELL SETEL

Sunday, October 20

Exodus 33:12–23/Isaiah 45:1–7

Psalm 99/Psalm 96:1–9 (10–13)

1 Thessalonians 1:1–10

Matthew 22:15–22

And God said, "My presence will go
with you, and I will give you rest."

—Exodus 33:14

*By **telling** our own **stories,** we can open our lives to God and to the community of other seekers. The process will gradually reach **back in time,** so we can learn to **love** those parts of our lives that seem unacceptable **today;** we may be able to love those parts of our **early lives** that seem to **threaten** us with bondage or hurt.*

— MARJORY ZOET BANKSON

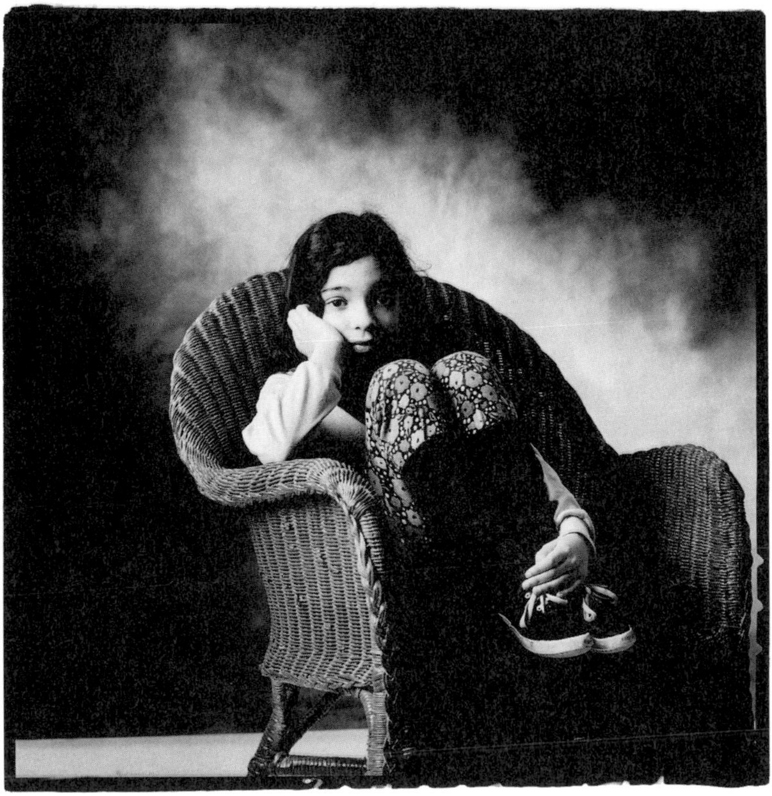

Geoffrey Pankhurst, Ayanna, ©1993

Monday, October 21

*For me the process of writing is
itself a time of joy.*

—BLANCHE WIESEN COOK

Tuesday, October 22

*Anger is a way to intimacy and
loving, if it is understood to contain
clues to our own pain.*

—RITA NAKASHIMA BROCK

Wednesday, October 23

Does my freedom to be myself
within the parameters of God's love
actually threaten to undo the
well-being of my community? No.
—CARTER HEYWARD

Thursday, October 24

We must keep our pens and
needles sharp against the cloak of
invisibility that our culture would
still like to fling over us.
—JANE MARCUS

Friday, October 25

The story of the human race begins

with the female.

—ROSALIND MILES

Saturday, October 26

Paul adopts the striking

image of himself as "nurse" to the

fledgling congregation.

—PHEME PERKINS

Sunday, October 27

DEUTERONOMY 34:1–12/LEVITICUS 19:1–2, 15–18

PSALM 90:1–6, 13–17/PSALM 1

1 THESSALONIANS 2:1–8

MATTHEW 22:34–46

But we were gentle among you,

like a nurse taking care of children.

—1 THESSALONIANS 2:7

*All theologies must be judged as to how far they contribute to the **liberation** and **humanization** of the human community. A living theology tries to bear witness to the unceasing yearning of human beings for **freedom** and **justice**, and articulates the human compassion for **peace** and **reconciliation**.*

—KWOK PUI-LAN

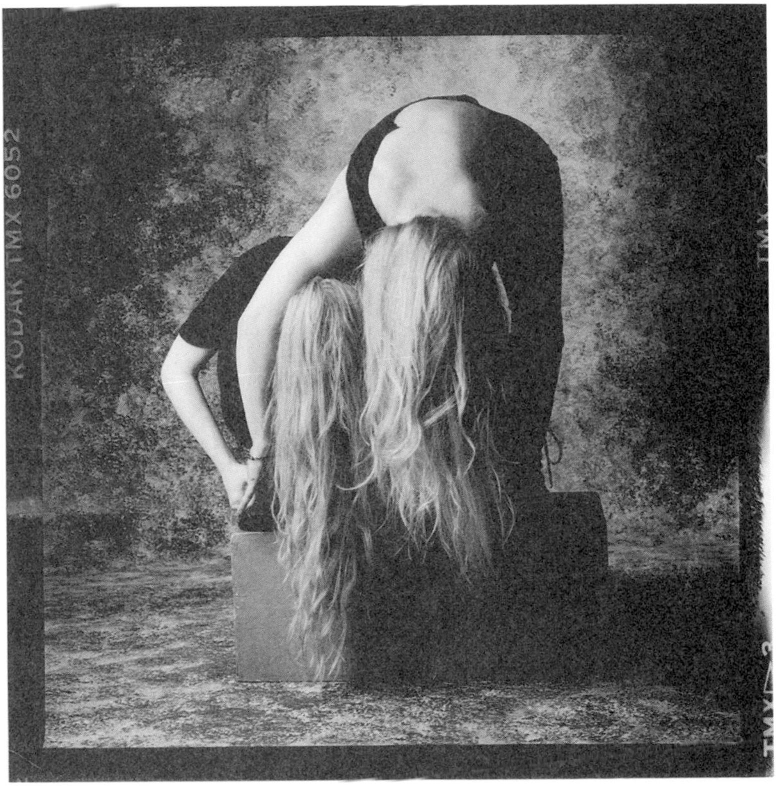
KODAK TMX 6052

Geoffrey Pankhurst, *The Eckles Twins*, ©1995

Monday, October 28

Silence is the most precious of mediums through which we can be initiated into the life of God.

—WENDY M. WRIGHT

Tuesday, October 29

What can specific women bring into our collective awareness? Above all, they can bring their sharp consciousness of pain.

—ANN BELFORD ULANOV

Wednesday, October 30

The compassionate God of the experience
of women means **a suffering God.**
—ANNE E. CARR

Thursday, October 31

HALLOWEEN

God's true voice within us respects
and honors our freedom.
—FLORA SLOSSON WUELLNER

Friday, November 1

*God heals us from self-seeking, that our
relationships may be honest and fulfilling.*

—LAVON BAYLER

Saturday, November 2

*[Matthew's] Gospel recognizes the
contributions made to the growth of the
church by women as well as by others
removed from positions of power.*

—AMY-JILL LEVINE

Sunday, November 3

JOSHUA 3:7-17/MICAH 3:5-12

PSALM 107:1-7, 33-37/PSALM 43

1 THESSALONIANS 2:9-13

MATTHEW 23:1-12

The one who is greatest among you shall be your servant; all who exalt themselves will be humbled, and all who humble themselves will be exalted.

—MATTHEW 23:11–12

We are human because we are jointly **responsible** with others for what happens to our **community.** In a community a person's **word** must be **heard** and **evaluated** alongside that of others. Gender is no criterion for the lack or possession of **wisdom.**

—MERCY AMBA ODUYOYE

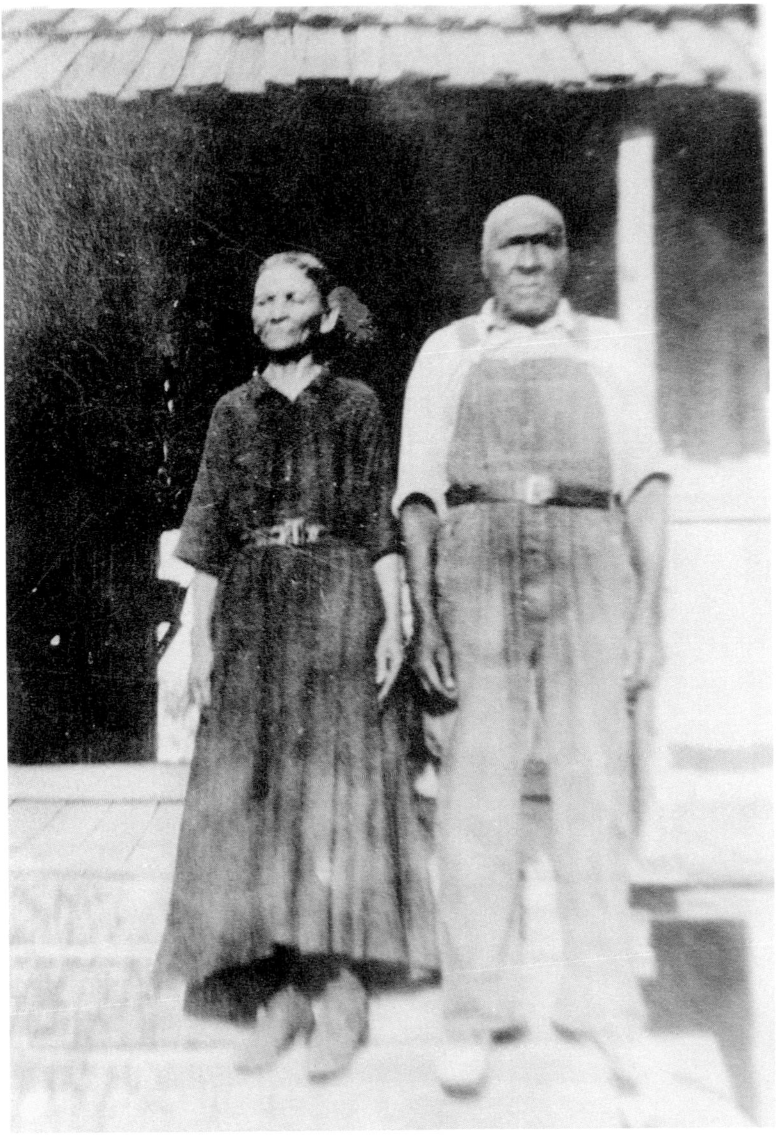

Courtesy of Alice R. Watson, Burton and Alice Strong, Marion, AL, ©1995

Monday, November 4

> *Our greatest sin . . . has always*
> *been our failure to take ourselves*
> *seriously as strong, powerful,*
> *autonomous and creative persons.*
>
> —CARTER HEYWARD

Tuesday, November 5

ELECTION DAY

> *Women should be tough, tender, laugh*
> *as much as possible, and live long lives.*
>
> —MAYA ANGELOU

Wednesday, November 6

Womankind has not been
mirrored in culture in ways that
provide us with adequate
and confident self-definition.
—BELL GALE CHEVIGNY

Thursday, November 7

Tender and compassionate God,
whose strength is made perfect
in our weakness, help us to believe
that you receive us as we are.
—RUTH C. DUCK

Friday, November 8

Women's art seeks meaning.

—JANE LAZARRE

Saturday, November 9

How do the faithful, overwhelmed
by danger, pain, or depression,
recognize that God is a trustworthy
presence in their midst?

—KATHLEEN A. FARMER

Sunday, November 10

But I am poor and needy;

hasten to me, O God!

You are my help and my deliverer;

O God, do not tarry!

—PSALM 70:5

*Even with **cultural self-expression** outlawed, my ancestors **never surrendered** their humanity or lost sight of a vision of freedom and justice they believed to be their due. . . . Against all odds, [African]-American slaves **created** a culture **saturated** with their own values and heavily laden with their **dreams.***

—KATIE GENEVA CANNON

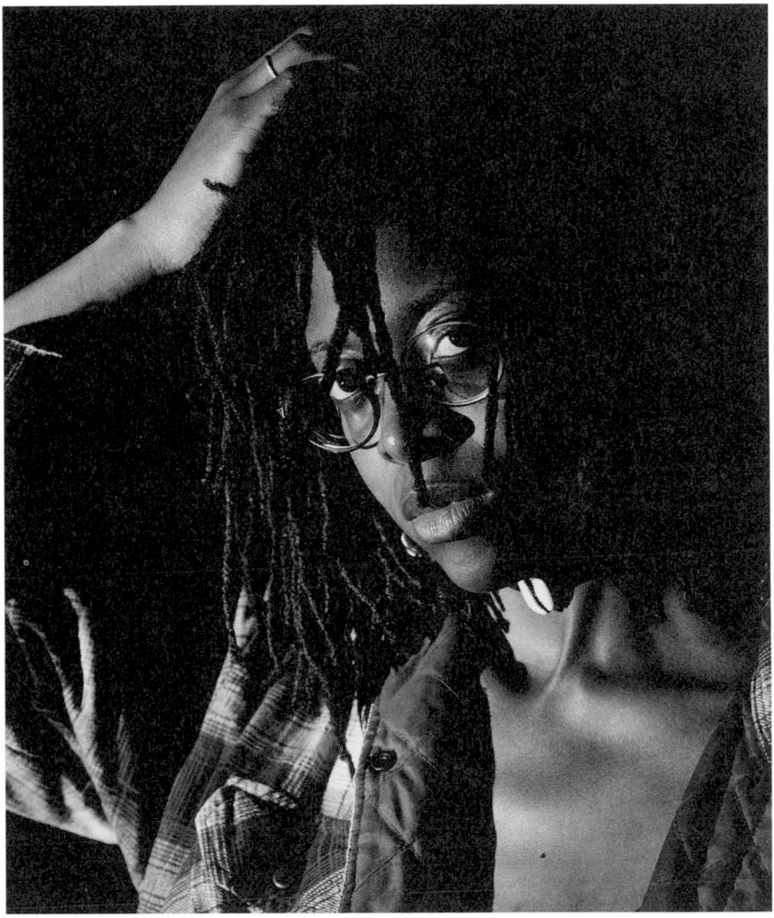

Amy Sorokas, *Untitled*, ©1994

Monday, November 11

> *Anger that we integrate, rather than*
> *vent on others, leads us to*
> *self-assertion and self-acceptance.*
> —RITA NAKASHIMA BROCK

Tuesday, November 12

> *I reach for my own words and*
> *hear my voice sent back, returning*
> *across a distance, reverberating*
> *with the lives of other women.*
> —JANET STERNBURG

Wednesday, November 13

Once we have embraced our
identity, our power gives us the
courage to accept others as they
choose to define themselves.
—PATRICIA L. HUNTER

Thursday, November 14

In Christ we are no longer
strangers and sojourners but dearly
loved children of the living God.
—MARY SUE GAST

Friday, November 15

Can you identify someone who
challenges you to grow without
invading your space? Who? How?
—MARJORY ZOET BANKSON

Saturday, November 16

"Wife of Lappidoth" could also be
translated "woman of fire," a
designation that says more about
Deborah's character than any
familial relationship implies.
—DANNA NOLAN FEWELL

JUDGES 4:1-7/ZEPHANIAH 1:7, 12-18

PSALM 123/PSALM 90:1-8 (9-11) 12

1 THESSALONIANS 5:1-11

MATTHEW 25:14-30

Now Deborah, a prophet, the wife

of Lappidoth, was judging Israel at

that time. She used to sit under the

palm of Deborah between Ramah

and Bethel in the hill country of

Ephraim; and the people of Israel

came up to her for judgment.

—JUDGES 4:4–5

*I was **born** a feminist on Thanksgiving weekend, 1975, when over one thousand Roman Catholic women met to insist on the right of women to be ordained to a renewed priestly ministry in our church. . . . But the process of **"giving birth to myself"** was not an all-of-a-sudden experience; in many ways the process had started **years before.***

—ADA MARÍA ISASI-DÍAZ

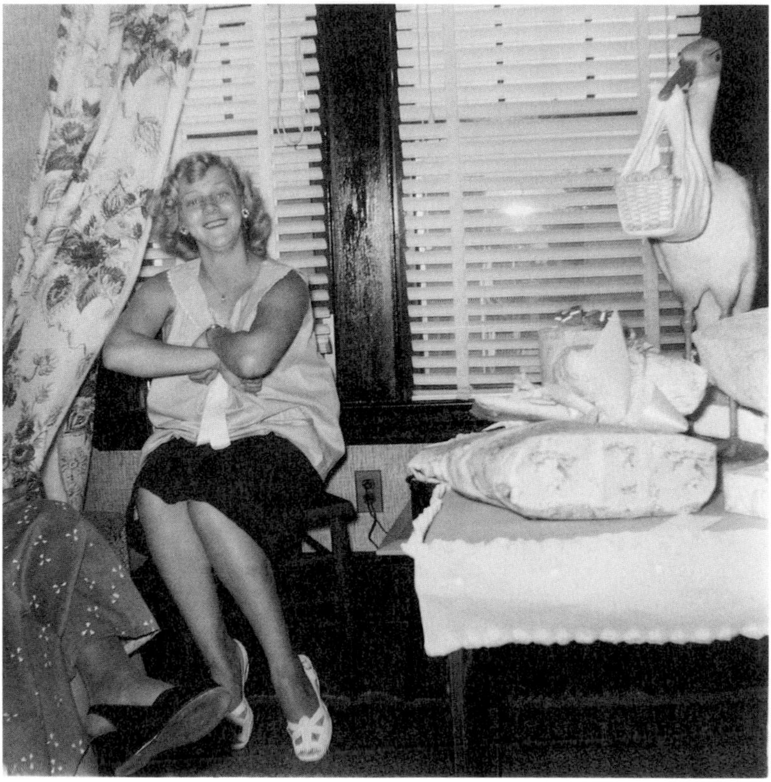

Thomas Jares, Arlene, ©1995

Monday, November 18

Spiritual friendship is
a profound act of hospitality.

—WENDY MILLER

Tuesday, November 19

Be strong women! Blush not!
Tremble not!

—SOJOURNER TRUTH

Wednesday, November 20

*It takes a lot of hard work and
courage to get to know who you are
and what you want.*

—SUE BENDER

Thursday, November 21

*I no longer see race and gender under
every tree—only under every other tree.*

—JOHNNETTA B. COLE

Friday, November 22

There are times to strategize and
times to ponder.

—DONNA SCHAPER

Saturday, November 23

Would or should women today want
to emulate their Israelite forebears?

—CAROL L. MEYERS

Sunday, November 24

EZEKIEL 34:11–16, 20–24/EZEKIEL 34:11–16, 20–24

PSALM 100/PSALM 95:1–7A

EPHESIANS 1:15–23

MATTHEW 25:31–46

I was hungry and you gave me food, I was thirsty and you gave me drink, I was a stranger and you welcomed me, I was naked and you clothed me, I was sick and you visited me, I was in prison and you came to me.

—MATTHEW 25:35–36

*Why do children **collect** feathers, hide gold paper, delicately perch a marble in the arms of an unresisting house plant, or stick shells under their beds or stones into their mattresses? The **"junk"** that is **precious** to children—and to adults— is precisely the stuff of the **sacred**.*

—LYNDA SEXSON

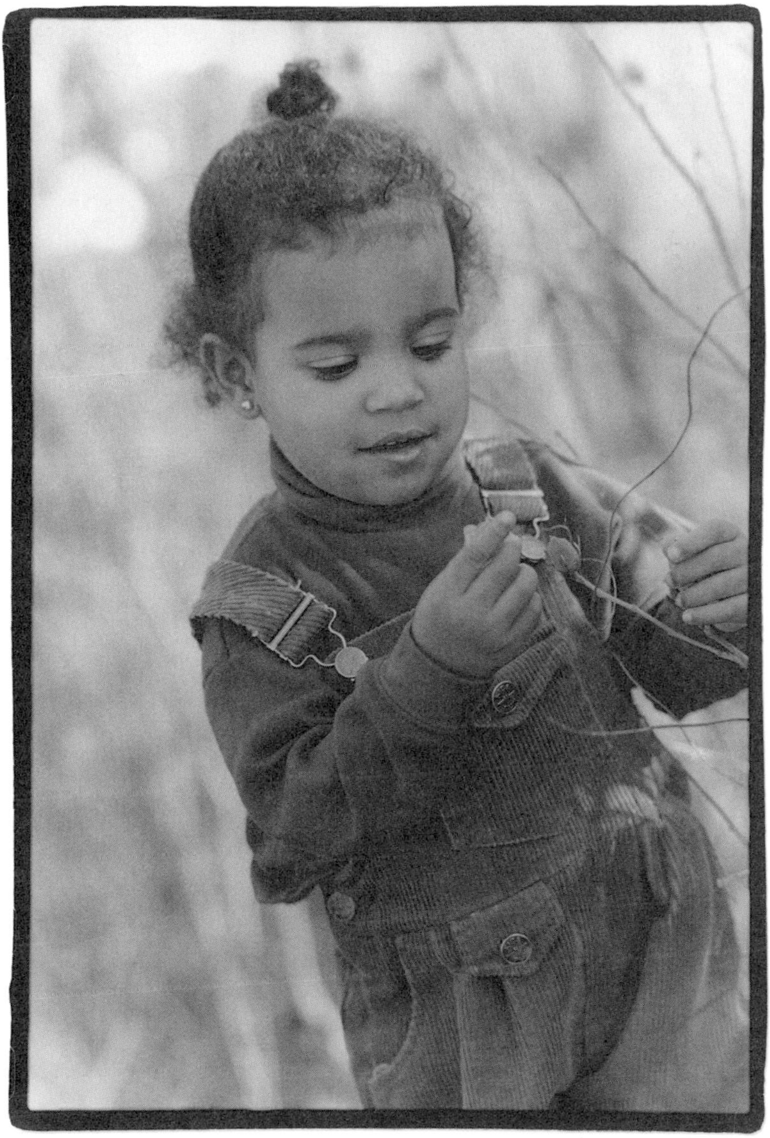

Leslie MacDonald, *Untitled*, ©1994

Monday, November 25

If I can stop one heart from breaking,
I shall not live in vain.
—EMILY DICKINSON

Tuesday, November 26

It is [children] who are God's presence,
promise, and hope for humankind.
—MARIAN WRIGHT EDELMAN

Wednesday, November 27

Home is a place to go out from,
to carry in the soul, and to return
to the imagination.
—CYNTHIA HIRNI

Thursday, November 28

THANKSGIVING DAY

There are few virtues more
beautiful than that of a spirit of
gratitude which asks for little and
is always thankful.
—PATRICIA E. DAVIS

Friday, November 29

What we in the church must be about, I am convinced, is a return to religion of passion.

—CARTER HEYWARD

Saturday, November 30

Women have found their own lives mirrored in the stories of quiet, valiant [biblical] women who experienced God's blessing on them.

—SHARON H. RINGE

Sunday, December 1

ISAIAH 64:1-9

PSALM 80:1-7, 17-19

1 CORINTHIANS 1:3-9

MARK 13:24-37

God is faithful, by whom you were

called into the community of God's

Child, Jesus Christ our Sovereign.

—1 CORINTHIANS 1:9

*That is why we **work so hard,** because we want to have the right **to determine** our lives rather than be dependent on others. We all are God's **children,** part of the whole creation, and **creation is sacred,** part of a holistic plan, where everybody and everything has an **important** role to play. Therefore, nothing should be wasted or mistreated, for everything is part of **life.***

— MARTA BENAVIDES

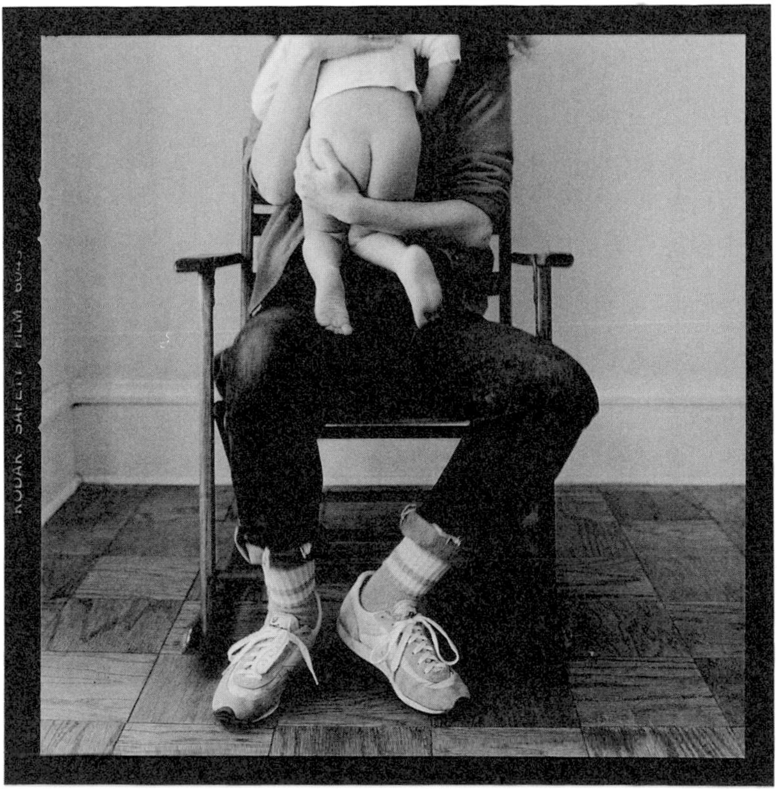
KODAK SAFETY FILM

Geoffrey Pankhurst, Untitled, ©1995

Monday, December 2

Native Americans have learned through harsh necessity that people who survive encroachment by another culture need story to survive.

—KATHLEEN NORRIS

Tuesday, December 3

Do the symbols, images, and language we use about God support or deny that which we claim to be our understanding of the nature of God?

—ANN McGREW BENNETT

Wednesday, December 4

Only with a principle of mutuality
can human persons truly be affirmed
as embodied subjects . . . as beings
whose destiny is communion.

—MARGARET A. FARLEY

Thursday, December 5

Associated with the feminine
element in all of us is a sense of
being-at-the-core-of-oneself.

—ANN BELFORD ULANOV

Friday, December 6

HANUKKAH

[A feminist moral theology] celebrates the reality that our moral-selves are body-selves which touch and see and hear each other into life.

—BEVERLY WILDUNG HARRISON

Saturday, December 7

I think that the dying pray at the last not "please," but "thank you."

—ANNIE DILLARD

Sunday, December 8

God will feed the flock like a shepherd,

gather the lambs in God's arms,

carry them in God's bosom,

and gently lead those that are with young.

—Isaiah 40:11

*I look on **aging** as the **gift of life,** and it is built into the divine plan of **creation.** History is certainly going somewhere, and we are either in the way of it or **on the way with it.** If it is the latter, then there is much to be accomplished.*

—ELIZABETH WELCH

Leslie MacDonald, *Grandma*, ©1994

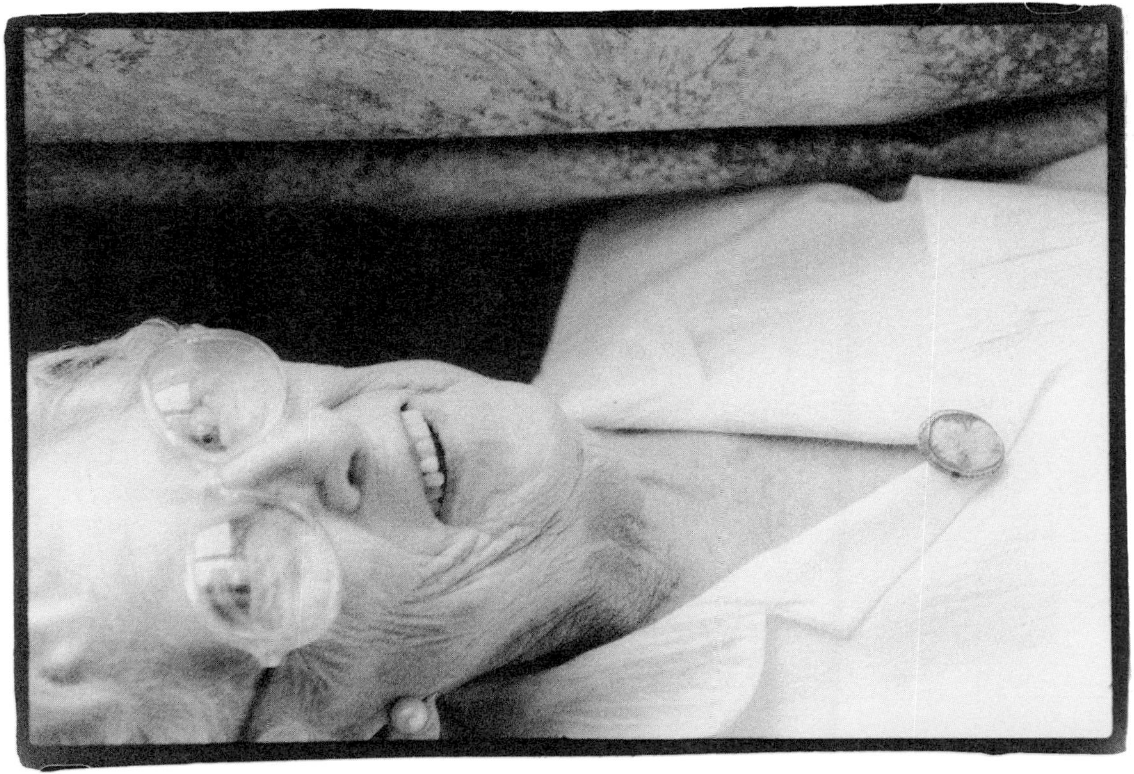

Monday, December 9

Mary, for Luke, is the exemplar of those who hear the word of God and keep it. It is for this reason that she makes possible God's messianic entrance into history.

—ROSEMARY RADFORD RUETHER

Tuesday, December 10

Many women inhabit the Hebrew Scriptures—powerful women, persuasive women.

—MIRIAM THERESE WINTER

Wednesday, December 11

*Many women have gotten their
first glimmer of liberation in the
community of faith.*

—NELLE MORTON

Thursday, December 12

*There is no impassable gulf
between the ways in which men
and women may look at
themselves and at their world.*

—VALERIE SAIVING

Friday, December 13

To see [Advent] only as a burden
and something which needs to be
rapidly rushed through is to lose a
depth of our Christian message.

—PATRICIA A. CARQUE

Saturday, December 14

What is at stake in developing
a feminist hermeneutic . . . in
relation to the Bible is, of course,
the interpretation of the biblical
witness as a whole.

—MARGARET A. FARLEY

Sunday, December 15

ISAIAH 61:1-4, 8-11

PSALM 126 (LUKE 1:47-55)

1 THESSALONIANS 5:16-24

JOHN 1:6-8, 19-28

When God restored the fortunes of Zion,

we were like those who dream.

Then our mouth was filled with laughter,

and our tongue with shouts of joy.

—PSALM 126:1–2

Jerry Mann, *Untitled*, ©1988

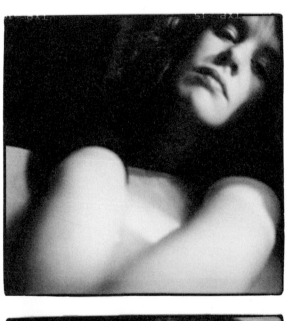

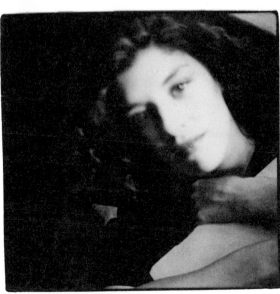

Monday, December 16

When we love ourselves and men
enough and are proud and angry
enough to come forth and refuse to
be oppressed one moment longer,
only then will we be credible.

—SONIA JOHNSON

Tuesday, December 17

As women have become more
self-conscious about themselves, their
relationship to authority, especially
religious authority, has changed.

—BARBARA BROWN ZIKMUND

Wednesday, December 18

As Woman-Church we claim the
authentic mission of Christ, the true
mission of Church, the real agenda of
our Mother-Father God who comes to
restore and not to destroy our humanity.
—ROSEMARY RADFORD RUETHER

Thursday, December 19

All efforts at self-transformation
challenge us to ongoing, critical
self-examination and reflection.
—BELL HOOKS

Friday, December 20

> Women cannot hoard the Christian
> virtues of humility, self-sacrifice,
> generosity, and modesty; neither can
> we reject the Christian virtues of
> leadership, decisive action, prophecy,
> strength, and assertion.
>
> —ALLA RENÉE BOZARTH

Saturday, December 21

> Within the admittedly patriarchal
> context of the biblical literature,
> we find strong countercurrents of
> affirmation of women.
>
> —J. CHERYL EXUM

Sunday, December 22

2 SAMUEL 7:1–11, 16

LUKE 1:47–55 (PSALM 89:1–4, 19–26)

ROMANS 16:25–27

LUKE 1:26–38

My soul magnifies the Sovereign,

and my spirit rejoices in God my Savior.

—LUKE 1:46–47

*My soul **magnifies** the Sovereign,*

*and my spirit **rejoices** in God my Savior,*

who has regarded the low estate of God's servant.

*For henceforth all generations will call me **blessed;***

*for the one who is mighty has done **great things** for me,*

and holy is God's name.

—LUKE 1:46B-49

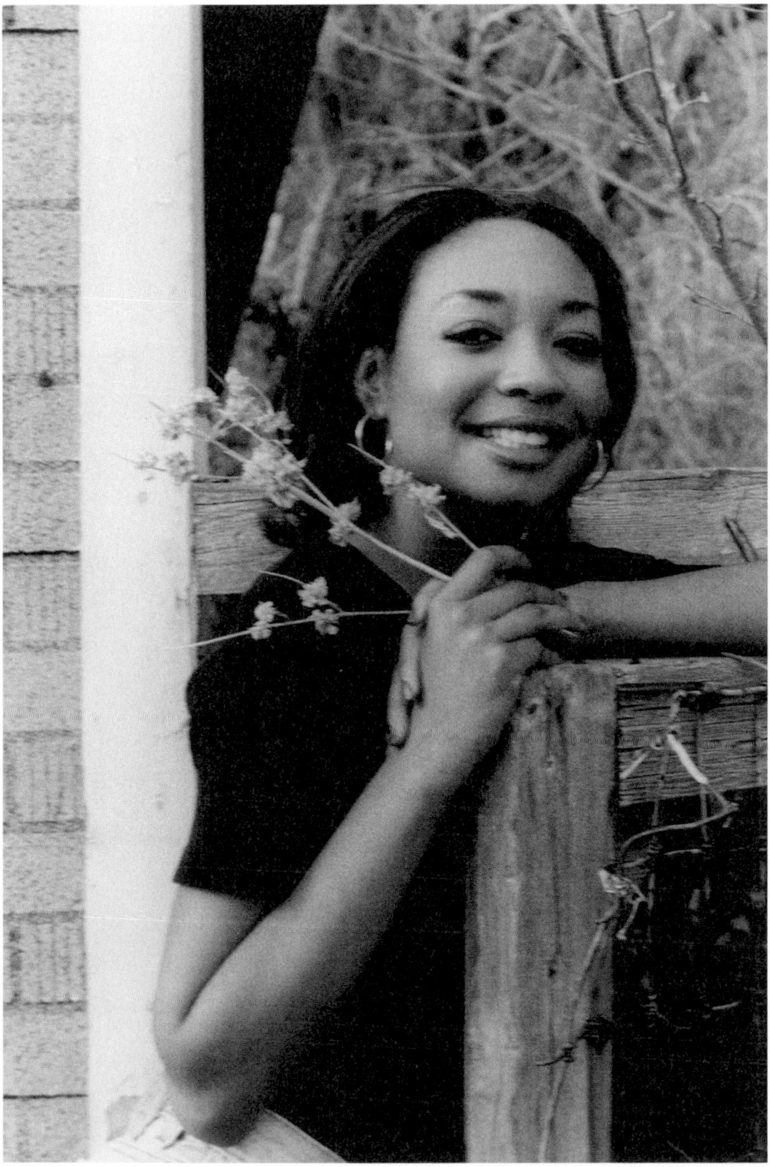

CLEO, *Urtitled*, ©1995

Monday, December 23

*[God's love is] a love characterized
by God's persistence throughout
human history in trying to rescue
us from our brokenness.*

—ROBERTA C. BONDI

Tuesday, December 24

CHRISTMAS EVE

*At Christmastime it is a season
for pondering on Mary's joyful
and sorrowful mysteries as they
are lived out anew by today's
women who are among the poorest
and the most abandoned.*

—MARGARET ELLEN TRAXLER

Wednesday, December 25

CHRISTMAS DAY

God has spoken to us by a Child,
by whose word the power of the
universe is upheld.
—LAVON BAYLER

Thursday, December 26

BOXING DAY (CANADA)

Be ablaze with enthusiasm.
Let us be an alive, burning offering
before the altar of God!
—HILDEGARD OF BINGEN

Friday, December 27

May She who creates peace in the
heavens create, in Her mercy, peace for
us and for all Israel, and say Amen.

—NAOMI JANOWITZ
AND MAGGIE WENIG

Saturday, December 28

We have to witness that there can
be an inclusive, loving, open liturgy.
. . . We have to share that with
other women—and men—of faith.

—BEATRICE PASTERNAK

Sunday, December 29

ISAIAH 61:10–62:3

PSALM 148

GALATIANS 4:4–7

LUKE 2:22–40

And coming up at that very hour [Anna] gave thanks to God, and spoke about the child to all who were looking for the redemption of Jerusalem.

—LUKE 2:38

In your **inner self** there are layers of collapse where violent upheavals have gone on, leaving you weak, unrestored, and vulnerable.

This is your **inner earth,** its slopes and plateaus, its reds, greens, pinks, deep down browns, and greys. You are **jagged** and **smooth** to touch, filled with **lights** and **shadows,** life and death. You are vast, complicated, unfinished, and **changing.**

—JOAN SAURO

Jerry Mann, *Untitled*, ©1988

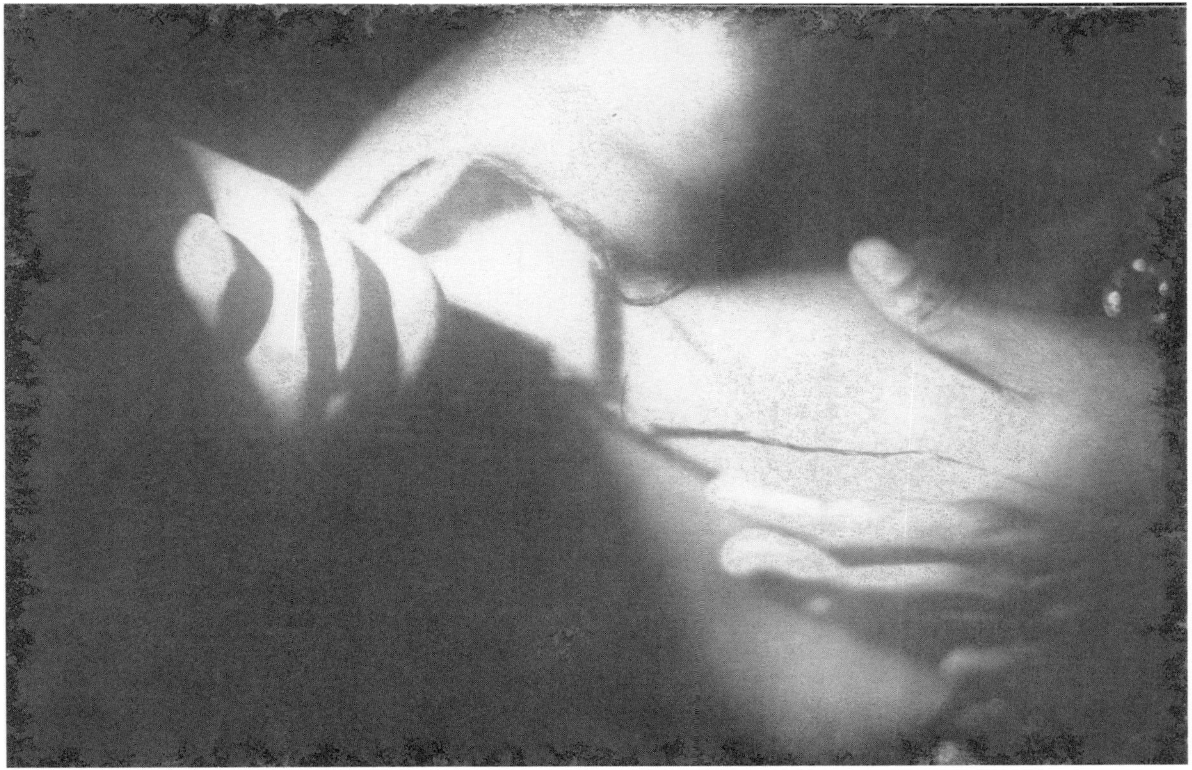

Monday, December 30

> *The diversity within feminist theology and spirituality is its strength.*
> —CAROL P. CHRIST
> AND JUDITH PLASKOW

Tuesday, December 31

> *Journal writing can be a way of taking ourselves seriously.*
> —ELAINE M. WARD

Wednesday, January 1

*People in our time find it hard
to accept the ebb and flow of life.
We prefer to see life as a logical
progression of events.*

—MARY D. KLAAREN

Thursday, January 2

*Any group that becomes sisterhood
starts because one or more women
recognize a mutual need.*

—MARY ZIMMER

Friday, January 3

> The unabridged woman is a female
> in process. She's growing; she's
> changing; she's trying to discover who
> she is and what she wants to be.
>
> —BOBBIE MCKAY

Saturday, January 4

> The people must be the ones
> to win, not the war, because war
> has nothing to do with humanity.
> War is something inhuman.
>
> —ZLATA FILIPOVIĆ

Sunday, January 5

Great is our God, and abundant in power,

with understanding beyond measure.

—PSALM 147:5

*God of **new** opportunities, you have opened for us a **fresh calendar** and **vast possibilities** for **new** experiences. Fill us now with your word of life, that we may dwell in your realm in this **new year.** Amen.*

—LAVON BAYLER

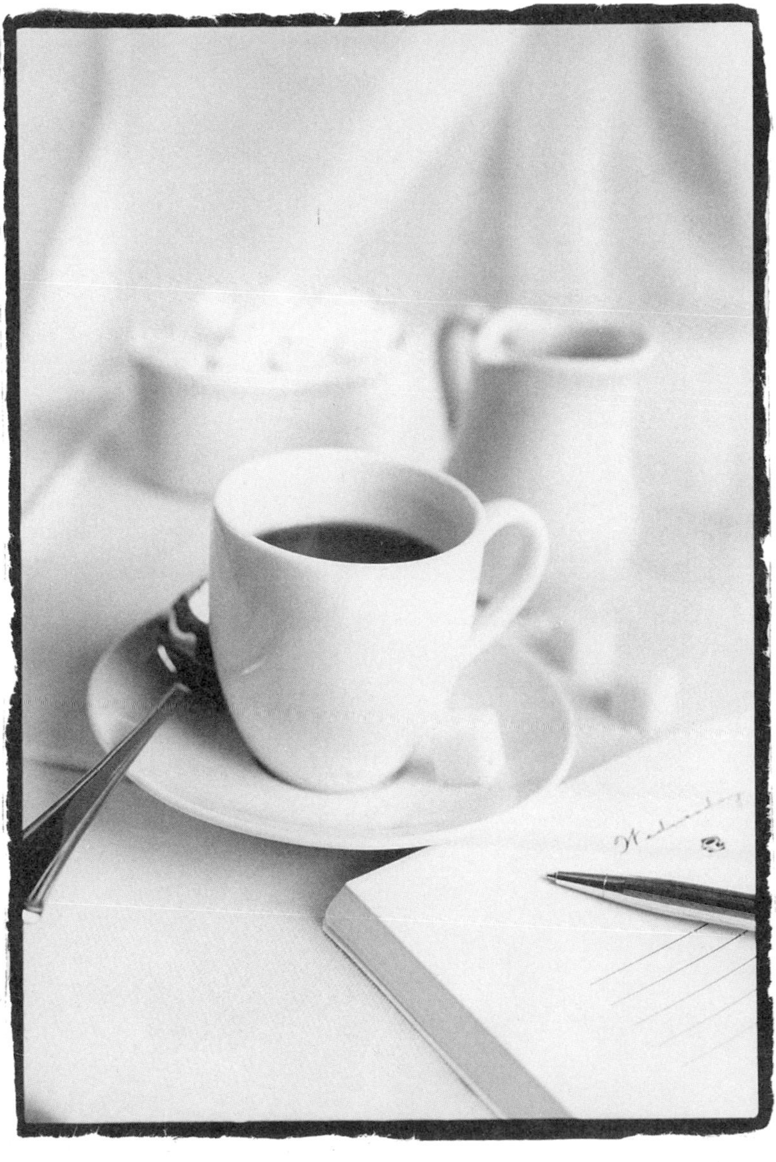

Jerry Mann, Untitled, ©1995

January

S	M	T	W	T	F	S
	1	2	3	4	5	6
7	8	9	10	11	12	13
14	15	16	17	18	19	20
21	22	23	24	25	26	27
28	29	30	31			

February

S	M	T	W	T	F	S
				1	2	3
4	5	6	7	8	9	10
11	12	13	14	15	16	17
18	19	20	21	22	23	24
25	26	27	28	29		

March

S	M	T	W	T	F	S
					1	2
3	4	5	6	7	8	9
10	11	12	13	14	15	16
17	18	19	20	21	22	23
$^{24}/_{31}$	25	26	27	28	29	30

April

S	M	T	W	T	F	S
	1	2	3	4	5	6
7	8	9	10	11	12	13
14	15	16	17	18	19	20
21	22	23	24	25	26	27
28	29	30				

May

S	M	T	W	T	F	S
			1	2	3	4
5	6	7	8	9	10	11
12	13	14	15	16	17	18
19	20	21	22	23	24	25
26	27	28	29	30	31	

June

S	M	T	W	T	F	S
						1
2	3	4	5	6	7	8
9	10	11	12	13	14	15
16	17	18	19	20	21	22
$^{23}/_{30}$	24	25	26	27	28	29

July

S	M	T	W	T	F	S
	1	2	3	4	5	6
7	8	9	10	11	12	13
14	15	16	17	18	19	20
21	22	23	24	25	26	27
28	29	30	31			

August

S	M	T	W	T	F	S
				1	2	3
4	5	6	7	8	9	10
11	12	13	14	15	16	17
18	19	20	21	22	23	24
25	26	27	28	29	30	31

September

S	M	T	W	T	F	S
1	2	3	4	5	6	7
8	9	10	11	12	13	14
15	16	17	18	19	20	21
22	23	24	25	26	27	28
29	30					

October

S	M	T	W	T	F	S
		1	2	3	4	5
6	7	8	9	10	11	12
13	14	15	16	17	18	19
20	21	22	23	24	25	26
27	28	29	30	31		

November

S	M	T	W	T	F	S
					1	2
3	4	5	6	7	8	9
10	11	12	13	14	15	16
17	18	19	20	21	22	23
24	25	26	27	28	29	30

December

S	M	T	W	T	F	S
1	2	3	4	5	6	7
8	9	10	11	12	13	14
15	16	17	18	19	20	21
22	23	24	25	26	27	28
29	30	31				

January

S	M	T	W	T	F	S
			1	2	3	4
5	6	7	8	9	10	11
12	13	14	15	16	17	18
19	20	21	22	23	24	25
26	27	28	29	30	31	

February

S	M	T	W	T	F	S
						1
2	3	4	5	6	7	8
9	10	11	12	13	14	15
16	17	18	19	20	21	22
23	24	25	26	27	28	

March

S	M	T	W	T	F	S
						1
2	3	4	5	6	7	8
9	10	11	12	13	14	15
16	17	18	19	20	21	22
$^{23}/_{30}$ $^{24}/_{31}$	25	26	27	28	29	

April

S	M	T	W	T	F	S
		1	2	3	4	5
6	7	8	9	10	11	12
13	14	15	16	17	18	19
20	21	22	23	24	25	26
27	28	29	30			

May

S	M	T	W	T	F	S
				1	2	3
4	5	6	7	8	9	10
11	12	13	14	15	16	17
18	19	20	21	22	23	24
25	26	27	28	29	30	31

June

S	M	T	W	T	F	S
1	2	3	4	5	6	7
8	9	10	11	12	13	14
15	16	17	18	19	20	21
22	23	24	25	26	27	28
29	30					

July

S	M	T	W	T	F	S
		1	2	3	4	5
6	7	8	9	10	11	12
13	14	15	16	17	18	19
20	21	22	23	24	25	26
27	28	29	30	31		

August

S	M	T	W	T	F	S
					1	2
3	4	5	6	7	8	9
10	11	12	13	14	15	16
17	18	19	20	21	22	23
24/31	25	26	27	28	29	30

September

S	M	T	W	T	F	S
	1	2	3	4	5	6
7	8	9	10	11	12	13
14	15	16	17	18	19	20
21	22	23	24	25	26	27
28	29	30				

October

S	M	T	W	T	F	S
			1	2	3	4
5	6	7	8	9	10	11
12	13	14	15	16	17	18
19	20	21	22	23	24	25
26	27	28	29	30	31	

November

S	M	T	W	T	F	S
						1
2	3	4	5	6	7	8
9	10	11	12	13	14	15
16	17	18	19	20	21	22
23/30	24	25	26	27	28	29

December

S	M	T	W	T	F	S
	1	2	3	4	5	6
7	8	9	10	11	12	13
14	15	16	17	18	19	20
21	22	23	24	25	26	27
28	29	30	31			

Bibliography

note: This is a listing of sources from which the quotes were taken. We have made every effort to find original sources, but were not able to do so in every case. In addition, we are aware that a few of these titles are out of print and no longer available for purchase.

Abernethy, Ann Greenwalt. "Unbinding for Life." See *Spinning a Sacred Yarn*.

Allen, Paula Gunn. "Grandmother of the Sun." See Judith Plaskow and Carol P. Christ.

Angelou, Maya. *I Know Why the Caged Bird Sings*. Bantam Books.

———. *Wouldn't Take Nothing for My Journey Now*. Random House.

Ascher, Carol, Louise DeSalvo, and Sara Ruddick, eds. *Between Women: Biographers, Novelists, Critics, Teachers and Artists Write About Their Work on Women*. Routledge.

Assaad, Marie. *Women, Religion and Sexuality: Studies on the Impact of Religious Teachings on Women*. Trinity Press International.

Bankson, Marjory Zoet. *Seasons of Friendship: Naomi and Ruth as a Pattern*. LuraMedia.

Bateson, Mary Catherine. *Composing a Life*. Plume.

Bayler, Lavon. *Fresh Winds of the Spirit: Liturgical Resources for Year A*. Pilgrim Press.

———. *Fresh Winds of the Spirit, Book 2: Liturgical Resources for Year A*. Pilgrim Press.

———. *Refreshing Rains of the Living Word: Liturgical Resources for Year C*. Pilgrim Press.

Benavides, Marta. "My Mother's Garden Is a New Creation." See Letty M. Russell et al.

Bender, Sue. *Plain and Simple: A Woman's Journey to the Amish*. HarperSanFrancisco.

Bennett, Ann McGrew. *From Woman-Pain to Women-Vision: Writings in Feminist Theology*. Augsburg Fortress.

Blomquist, Jean M. *Wrestling till Dawn: Awakening to Life in Times of Struggle*.

Upper Room Books.

Bondi, Roberta C. "Becoming Bearers of Reconciliation." In *Weavings: A Journal of the Christian Spiritual Life,* vol. 5, no. 1 (January/February 1990). The Upper Room.

———. "The Paradox of Prayer." In *Weavings: A Journal of the Christian Spiritual Life,* vol. 4, no. 2 (March/April 1989). The Upper Room.

Bozarth, Alla Renée. *Womanpriest: A Personal Odyssey.* LuraMedia.

Brock, Rita Nakashima. *Journeys by Heart: A Christology of Erotic Power.* Crossroad.

———. "On Mirrors, Mists, and Murmurs." See Judith Plaskow and Carol P. Christ.

Brown, Lyn Mikel, and Carol Gilligan. *Meeting at the Crossroads: Women's Psychology and Girls' Development.* Harvard University Press.

Broyles, Anne. *Growing Together in Love: God Known Through Family Life.* Upper Room Books.

Cannon, Katie Geneva. "Surviving the Blight." See Letty M. Russell et al.

———. "The Emergence of Black Feminist Consciousness." See Letty M. Russell, ed.

Carlson, Carole. "America—Finished or Unfinished." See *Spinning a Sacred Yarn.*

Carque, Patricia A. "The Wait of Pregnancy." See *Spinning a Sacred Yarn.*

Carr, Anne E. *Transforming Grace: Christian Tradition and Women's Experience.* HarperSanFrancisco.

Carroll, Maureen P. "A Homily for the Feast of Teresa of Avila, Doctor of the Church." See *Spinning a Sacred Yarn.*

Chase, Carole F., "Redemption." See *Readings for Lent and Easter.*

Chernin, Kim. *Reinventing Eve: Modern Woman in Search of Herself.* Harper & Row.

Chevigny, Bell Gale. "Daughters Writing: Toward a Theory of Women's Biography." See Carol Ascher et al.

Christ, Carol P. *Laughter of Aphrodite: Reflections of a Journey to the Goddess.* Harper & Row.

———. "Spiritual Quest and Women's Experience." See Carol P. Christ and Judith Plaskow.

Christ, Carol P., and Judith Plaskow, eds. *Womanspirit Rising: A Feminist Reader in Religion.* Harper & Row.

Clark, Linda. "The Day's Own Trouble." See *Spinning a Sacred Yarn.*

Clowse, Barbara Barksdale. *Women, Decision Making, and the Future.* John Knox Press.

Cole, Johnnetta B. *Conversations: Straight Talk with America's Sister President.* Anchor Books.

Collins, Sheila. "Reflections on the Meaning of Herstory." See Carol P. Christ and Judith Plaskow.

Cook, Blanche Wiesen. "Biographer and Subject: A Critical Connection." See Carol Ascher et al.

Crockett-Cannon, Margaret W. "What Do You Want Me to Do for You?" See *Spinning a Sacred Yarn.*

Crosby, Harriet E. "Literary Saints and Mystics." In *Weavings: A Journal of the Christian Spiritual Life,* vol. 3, no. 5 (September/October 1988). The Upper Room.

Daly, Mary. "After the Death of God the Father" See Judith Plaskow and Carol P. Christ.

———. "Be-Friending." See Judith Plaskow and Carol P. Christ.

———. *Beyond God the Father: Toward a Philosophy of Women's Liberation.* Beacon Press.

———. "Why Speak About God?" See Carol P. Christ and Judith Plaskow.

Darr, Katheryn Pfisterer. *Far More Precious Than Jewels: Perspectives on Biblical Women.* Westminster/John Knox Press.

Daum, Annette. " 'Sisterhood' Is Powerful." See *Spinning a Sacred Yarn.*

Davies, Susan E., and Eleanor H. Haney, eds., *Religion and Sexual Ethics: A Sourcebook of Essays, Stories, and Poems.* Pilgrim Press.

Davis, Patricia E. "The Best Is Yet to Be." See *Spinning a Sacred Yarn.*

Denham, Priscilla. "It's Hard to Sing the Song of Deborah." See *Spinning a Sacred Yarn.*

Denman, Rose Mary. *Let My People In: A Lesbian Minister Tells of Her Struggles to Live Openly and Maintain Her Ministry.* William Morrow.

Desert Mother Syncletica. *Sayings of the Desert Mothers Sarah, Syncletica, and Theodora.* Macmillan.

Dickinson, Emily, *The Poems of Emily Dickinson.* Little, Brown and Company.

Dillard, Annie. *Pilgrim at Tinker Creek.* Harper's Magazine Press.

———. *The Writing Life.* Harper & Row.

Dinesen, Isak. *Babette's Feast and Other Anecdotes of Destiny.* Vintage Books.

Donnelly, Doris. "Good Tidings of Great Joy," in *Weavings: A Journal of the Christian Spiritual Life,* vol. 8, no. 6 (November/December 1993). The Upper Room.

Duck, Ruth C. *Gender and the Name of God: The Trinitarian Baptismal Formula.* Pilgrim Press.

———, ed. *Bread for the Journey: Resources for Worship.* Pilgrim Press.

Eakin, Joann Nash. "From the Prairie to the World." See Letty M. Russell et al.

Edelman, Marian Wright. *The Measure of Our Success: A Letter to My Children and Yours.* Beacon Press.

Ellerbee, Linda. *Move On: Adventures in the Real World.* HarperCollins.

Eslinger, Elise S. *The Upper Room Worshipbook.* Upper Room Books.

Exum, J. Cheryl. "Mother in Israel: A Familiar Figure Reconsidered." See Letty M. Russell, ed.

Falk, Marcia. "Notes on Composing New Blessings." See Judith Plaskow and Carol P. Christ.

Farley, Margaret A. "Feminist Consciousness and the Interpretation of Scripture." See Letty M. Russell, ed.

Farmer, Kathleen A. "Psalms." See Carol A. Newsom and Sharon H. Ringe.

Fewell, Danna Nolan. "Joshua, Judges." See Carol A. Newsom and Sharon H. Ringe.

Filipovic, Zlata. *Zlata's Diary: A Child's Life in Sarajevo.* Viking Penguin.

Fiorenza, Elisabeth Schüssler. "Feminist Spirituality, Christian Identity, and Catholic Vision." See Carol P. Christ and Judith Plaskow.

———. "In Search of Women's Heritage." See Judith Plaskow and Carol P. Christ.

———. "The Will to Choose or to Reject: Continuing Our Critical Work." See Letty M. Russell, ed.

———. "Women in the Early Christian Movement." See Carol P. Christ and Judith Plaskow.

Fortune, Marie M. "My God, My God, Why Have You Forsaken Me?" See *Spinning a Sacred Yarn.*

Frank, Margie M. "How Can This Be?" See *Spinning a Sacred Yarn.*

Froehle, Virginia Ann. *Called into Her Presence: Praying with Feminine Images of God.* Ave Maria Press.

Gast, Mary Susan. See Ruth Duck, ed.

Geller, Laura. "Can Isaac and Ishmael Be Reconciled?" See *Spinning a Sacred Yarn.*

Gilligan, Carol. *In a Different Voice:*

Psychological Theory and Women's Development. Harvard University Press.

Goldberg, Natalie. *Writing Down the Bones: Freeing the Writer Within.* Shambhala.

Gonzalez, Catherine Gunsalus. "Standing in God's Presence." See *Readings for Lent and Easter.*

Greenberg, Blu. In Jeanne Becher, ed., *Women, Religion, and Sexuality: Studies on the Impact of Religious Teachings on Women.* Trinity Press International.

Griffin, Susan. "The Earth Is My Sister." See Judith Plaskow and Carol P. Christ.

Grindal, Gracia. "Both Boxes." See *Spinning a Sacred Yarn.*

Gross, Rita M. "Female God Language in a Jewish Context." See Carol P. Christ and Judith Plaskow.

Gudorf, Christine E. *Body, Sex, and Pleasure: Reconstructing Christian Sexual Ethics.* Pilgrim Press.

Gustafson, Jamie R. "Dry Bones and Rolled Stones." See *Spinning a Sacred Yarn.*

Hadewijch: The Complete Works. Paulist Press.

Halkes, Catharina J. M. *New Creation: Christian Feminism and the Renewal of the Earth.* Westminster/John Knox Press.

Hammond, Pixie Roestline. "Forgiveness." See *Readings for Lent and Easter.*

Hancock, Eugenia Lee. "The Impatience of Job." See *Spinning a Sacred Yarn.*

Haney, Eleanor H. "Sexual Being: Burden and Possibility." See Susan E. Davies and Eleanor H. Haney.

Harkness, Georgia. In Rosemary Skinner Keller, ed., *Georgia Harkness: For Such a Time as This.* Abingdon Press.

Harris, Maria. *Fashion Me a People: Curriculum in the Church.* Westminster/John Knox Press.

Harrison, Beverly Wildung. "The Power of Anger in the Work of Love." See Judith Plaskow and Carol P. Christ.

Heyward, Carter. "The Enigmatic God." See *Spinning a Sacred Yarn.*

———. *Our Passion for Justice: Images of Power, Sexuality, and Liberation.* Pilgrim Press.

———. *Speaking of Christ: A Lesbian Feminist Voice.* Pilgrim Press.

Hickman, Martha Whitmore. *Fullness of Time: Short Stories of Women and Aging.* Upper Room Books.

Hildegard of Bingen. *Meditations with Hildegard of Bingen.* Bear & Co.

Hillesum, Etty. *An Interrupted Life: The Diaries of Etty Hillesum, 1941-43.* Washington Square Press.

Hirni, Cynthia. *The Ridge Leaf.* May 1994. Kirkridge, Bangor, PA 18013.

Hooks, Bell. *Talking Back: Thinking Feminist, Thinking Black.* South End Press.

Hughes, Kathleen. In Barbara Bowe, Kathleen Hughes, Sharon Karam, and Carolyn Osiek, eds. *Silent Voices, Sacred Lives: Women's Readings for the Liturgical Year.* Paulist Press.

Hull, Gloria T. "Alice Dunbar-Nelson: A Personal and Literary Perspective." See Carol Ascher et al.

Hunt, Mary E. "You Do, I Don't." See Susan E. Davies and Eleanor H. Haney.

Hunter, Patricia L. "Women's Power— Women's Passion." In Emilie M. Townes, ed., *A Troubling in My Soul.* Orbis Books.

Isasi-Díaz, Ada María. "A Hispanic Garden in a Foreign Land." See Letty M. Russell et al.

Jacobson, Jodi L. "Closing the Gender Gap in Development." In *State of the*

World 1993: A Worldwatch Institute
Report on Progress Toward a Sustainable
Society. W. W. Norton.

Janowitz, Naomi, and Maggie Wenig.
"Sabbath Prayers for Women." See
Carol P. Christ and Judith Plaskow.

Johnson, Elizabeth A. She Who Is: The
Mystery of God in Feminist Theological
Discourse. Crossroad.

Johnson, Sonia. From Housewife to
Heretic: One Woman's Struggle for
Equal Rights and Her Excommunication
from the Mormon Church. Doubleday.

Juengst, Sara Covin. Breaking Bread: The
Spiritual Significance of Food.
Westminster/John Knox Press.

Julian of Norwich. Showings. Paulist
Press.

Kauffman, Janet. Collaborators. Graywolf
Press.

Keller, Rosemary. "This Ministry: God's
Mercy . . . Our Hope." See Spinning a
Sacred Yarn.

Klaaren, Mary D. "Realism and Hope."
See Spinning a Sacred Yarn.

Koller, Alice. The Stations of Solitude.
Bantam Books.

Koolish, Lynda. "This Is Who She Is to
Me: On Photographing Women." See
Carol Ascher et al.

Lane, Ann J. "Do Women Have a
History? Reassessing the Past and
Present" In Patricia Altenbernd
Johnson and Janet Kalven, eds., With
Both Eyes Open: Seeing Beyond
Gender. Pilgrim Press.

Lazarre, Jane. " 'Charlotte's Web':
Reading Jane Eyre over Time." See
Carol Ascher et al.

Levine, Amy-Jill. "Matthew." See Carol
A. Newsom and Sharon H. Ringe.

Lorde, Audre. "Uses of the Erotic." See
Judith Plaskow and Carol P. Christ.

Lunneen, Sally. "Women: Living
Wholly/Holy in a Fractured World."
See Spinning a Sacred Yarn.

Marcus, Jane. "Invisible Mending." See
Carol Ascher et al.

McFague, Sallie. The Body of God: An
Ecological Theology. Fortress Press.

———. Speaking in Parables: A Study in
Metaphor and Theology. Fortress Press.

McGee, Mary. "In Celebration of
Heroes and Nobodies." See Spinning
a Sacred Yarn.

McKay, Bobbie. The Unabridged Woman.
The Pilgrim Press.

McLaughlin, Eleanor L. "The Christian
Past: Does It Hold a Future for
Women?" See Carol P. Christ and
Judith Plaskow.

Meyers, Carol L. "Everyday Life:
Women in the Period of the Hebrew
Bible." See Carol A. Newsom and
Sharon H. Ringe.

Miles, Rosalind. The Women's History of
the World. Salem House.

Miller, Wendy. Learning to Listen: A
Guide for Spiritual Friends. Upper
Room Books.

Mollenkott, Virginia Ramey. "The
Ephesians Vision: Universal Justice."
See Spinning a Sacred Yarn.

———. "Interreligious Dialogue: A
Pilgrimage." In Daughters of Sarah:
The Magazine for Christian Feminists,
vol. 20, no. 2 (Spring 1994).

———. Speech, Silence, Action!
Abingdon Press.

Moltmann-Wendel, Elisabeth. A Land
Flowing with Milk and Honey:
Perspectives on Feminist Theology.
Crossroad.

Morton, Nelle. "The Dilemma of
Celebration." See Carol P. Christ and
Judith Plaskow.

———. The Journey Is Home. Beacon
Press.

Mother Teresa. A Gift for God. Harper
& Row.

Nelson, Christine. "Job: The
Confessions of a Suffering Person."
See Spinning a Sacred Yarn.

Newsom, Carol A., and Sharon H. Ringe, eds. *The Women's Bible Commentary*. Westminster Press.

Niebuhr, Hulda. In Elizabeth Caldwell, *A Mysterious Mantle: The Biography of Hulda Niebuhr*. Pilgrim Press.

Norris, Kathleen. *Dakota: A Spiritual Geography*. Ticknor & Fields.

Oduyoye, Mercy Amba. "Be a Woman, and Africa Will Be Strong." See Letty M. Russell et al.

O'Connor, Flannery. *Mystery and Manners: Occasional Prose*. Farrar, Strauss, & Giroux.

O'Reilley, Mary Rose. "Deep Listening: An Experimental Friendship." In *Weavings: A Journal of the Christian Spiritual Life,* vol. 9, no. 3 (May/June 1994). The Upper Room.

Palmer, Sally. "The Wounded Healer." See *Spinning a Sacred Yarn*.

Pasternak, Beatrice. "Created in Her Image." See *Spinning a Sacred Yarn*.

Pearson, Helen Bruch. *Do What You Have the Power to Do: Studies of Six New Testament Women*. Upper Room Books.

Perkins, Pheme. "Philippians; 1 Thessalonians." See Carol A. Newsom and Sharon H. Ringe.

Plaskow, Judith. "The Coming of Lilith: Toward a Feminist Theology." See Carol P. Christ and Judith Plaskow.

Plaskow, Judith, and Carol P. Christ, eds., *Weaving the Visions: New Patterns in Feminist Spirituality*. HarperSanFrancisco.

Pogrebin, Letty Cottin. "Competing with Women." In Valerie Miner and Helen E. Longino, eds., *Competition: A Feminist Taboo?* Feminist Press.

Pui-lan, Kwok. "Mothers and Daughters, Writers and Fighters." See Letty M. Russell et al.

Quindlen, Anna. *Thinking Out Loud: On the Personal, the Political, the Public and the Private*. Fawcett Columbine.

Ransom, Gail S. "Chafing Dish, Apron Strings." See *Spinning a Sacred Yarn*.

Rayburn, Carole A. "Three Women from Moab." See *Spinning a Sacred Yarn*.

Readings for Lent and Easter from The Upper Room. Upper Room Books.

Richardson, Beth A. "Journey Without End." See *Readings for Lent and Easter*.

Riggs, Marcia Y. *Awake, Arise, and Act: A Womanist Call for Black Liberation*. Pilgrim Press.

———. "The Logic of Interstructured Oppression." See Susan E. Davies and Eleanor H. Haney.

Ringe, Sharon H. "A Gentile Woman's Story." See Letty M. Russell, ed.

———. "When Women Interpret the Bible." See Carol A. Newsom and Sharon H. Ringe.

Roberts, Nanette. "Last at the Cross." See *Spinning a Sacred Yarn*.

Ruddick, Sara. "New Combinations: Learning from Virginia Woolf." See Carol Ascher et al.

Ruether, Rosemary Radford. "Feminist Interpretation: A Method of Correlation." See Letty M. Russell, ed.

———. "Mother Earth and the Megamachine." See Carol P. Christ and Judith Plaskow.

———. "Woman as Oppressed; Woman as Liberated in the Scriptures." See *Spinning a Sacred Yarn*.

———. *Womanguides: Readings Toward a Feminist Theology*. Beacon Press.

Russell, Letty M. "Authority and the Challenge of Feminist Interpretation." See Letty M. Russell, ed.

———. *Human Liberation in a Feminist Perspective: A Theology*. Westminster/John Knox Press.

———, ed. *Feminist Interpretation of the Bible*. Westminster Press.

Russell, Letty M., Kwok Pui-lan, Ada Maria Isasi-Diaz, Katie Geneva Cannon, eds. *Inheriting Our Mothers' Gardens: Feminist Theology in Third World Perspective.* Westminster Press.

Sackenfeld, Katharine Doob. "Feminist Uses of Biblical Materials." See Letty M. Russell, ed.

Saiving, Valerie. "The Human Situation: A Feminine View." See Carol P. Christ and Judith Plaskow.

Sauro, Joan. "The Whole Earth Meditation." In *Weavings: A Journal of the Christian Spiritual Life,* vol. 6, no. 6 (November/December 1991). The Upper Room.

Saussy, Carroll. *God Images and Self-Esteem: Empowering Women in a Patriarchal Society.* Westminster/John Knox Press.

Sawatzky, Sharon Blessum. "Sometimes There's God, So Quickly." See *Spinning a Sacred Yarn.*

Schaper, Donna. "Rabbits in Winter." See *Readings for Lent and Easter.*

———. In *Manna: A Daily Devotional for Activists.* Winter 1994. 165 West Street, Amherst, MA, 01002.

———. "The Movement of Suffering." See *Spinning a Sacred Yarn.*

Schaudt, Yvonne V. "Frontiers." See *Spinning a Sacred Yarn.*

Schneiders, Sandra M. *Women and the Word: The Gender of God in the New Testament and the Spirituality of Women.* Paulist Press.

Scroggs, Marilee. See Ruth C. Duck, ed.

Setel, Drorah O'Donnell. "Exodus." See Carol A. Newsom and Sharon H. Ringe.

Sexson, Lynda. *Ordinarily Sacred.* University Press of Virginia.

Smiley, Jane. *At Paradise Gate.* Simon & Schuster.

Smith, Christine M. *Weaving the Sermon: Preaching in a Feminist Perspective.* Westminster/John Knox Press.

Smith, Judith E. "The One Thing Necessary." In *Weavings: A Journal of the Christian Spiritual Life,* vol. 3, no. 3 (May/June 1988). The Upper Room.

Sölle, Dorothee. *Thinking About God: An Introduction to Theology.* Trinity Press International.

Spencer, Sue Nichols. *Renewing the Vision: Daily Readings for Peacemakers.* Westminster/John Knox Press.

Spinning a Sacred Yarn: Women Speak from the Pulpit. Pilgrim Press.

Steinem, Gloria. *Moving Beyond Words.* Simon & Schuster.

Sternberg, Janet. "Farewell to the Farm." See Carol Ascher et al.

Stetson, Erlene. "Silence: Access and Aspiration." See Carol Ascher et al.

Tannen, Deborah. *You Just Don't Understand: Women and Men in Conversation.* Morrow.

Taylor, Barbara Brown. "A Great Cloud of Witnesses." In *Weavings: A Journal of the Christian Spiritual Life,* vol. 3, no. 5 (September/October 1988). The Upper Room.

Tennis, Diane. "Suffering." See *Spinning a Sacred Yarn.*

Thibault, Jane Marie. *A Deepening Love Affair: The Gift of God in Later Life.* Upper Room Books.

Thistlethwaite, Susan Brooks. "Every Two Minutes: Battered Women and Feminist Interpretation." See Letty M. Russell, ed.

Thompson, Marjorie J. "Moving Toward Forgiveness." In *Weavings: A Journal of the Christian Spiritual Life,* vol. 7, no. 2 (March/April 1992). The Upper Room.

———. "The Heart of Christian Paradox." In *Upper Room Disciplines 1990.* Upper Room Books.

Tickle, Phyllis. *Final Sanity.* Upper

Room Books.

Traxler, Margaret Ellen. "Mary's Christmas Announces Freedom to Captives." See *Spinning a Sacred Yarn*.

Trebbi, Diana. "My Prayer 'Grows Up' as I Grow Older." See *Spinning a Sacred Yarn*.

Trible, Phyllis. "Eve and Adam: Genesis 2-3 Reread." See Carol P. Christ and Judith Plaskow.

———. "Postscript: Jottings on the Journey." See Letty M. Russell, ed.

———. *Texts of Terror: Literary-Feminist Readings of Biblical Narratives*. Fortress Press.

Trible, Phyllis, and Elisabeth Fiorenza. See Carol P. Christ and Judith Plaskow, eds.

Truth, Sojourner. "I Want Women to Have Their Rights . . . I Will Shake Every Place I Go To." In *Historic Speeches of African Americans*. Franklin Watts.

Ulanov, Ann Belford. *Receiving Woman: Studies in the Psychology and Theology of the Feminine*. Westminster Press.

Walker, Alice. *In Search of Our Mothers' Gardens: Womanist Prose*. Harcourt Brace Jovanovich.

Ward, Elaine M. *Bread for the Banquet: Experiencing Life in the Spirit*. United Church Press.

Way, Peggy. "You Are Not My God, Jehovah." See *Spinning a Sacred Yarn*.

Weems, Ann. *Reaching for Rainbows: Resources for Creative Worship*. Westminster Press.

Weil, Simone. *Waiting for God*. G. P. Putnam's Sons.

Welch, Elizabeth. *Learning to Be 85*. Upper Room Books.

Werth, Terry. "Today Is All We Have." See *Spinning a Sacred Yarn*.

White, Alma. In Susie Cunningham Stanley, *Feminist Pillar of Fire: The Life of Alma White*. Pilgrim Press.

Williams, Delores S. "Womanist Theology." See Judith Plaskow and Carol P. Christ.

Williams, Terry Tempest. *Refuge*. Vintage Books.

Winter, Miriam Therese. *Woman Wisdom: A Feminist Lectionary and Psalter*. Crossroad.

Woolf, Virginia. *A Room of One's Own*. Harcourt Brace Jovanovich.

———. *Three Guineas*. Harcourt Brace Jovanovich.

Wright, Wendy M. *The Vigil: Keeping Watch in the Season of Christ's Coming*. Upper Room Books.

Wuellner, Flora Slosson. *Prayer, Fear, and Our Powers: Finding Our Healing, Release, and Growth in Christ*. Upper Room Books.

———. "When Prayer Encounters Pain." In *Weavings: A Journal of the Christian Spiritual Life*, vol. 4, no. 3 (May/June 1989). The Upper Room.

Zikmund, Barbara Brown. "Feminist Consciousness in Historical Perspective." See Letty M. Russell, ed.

Zimmer, Mary. *Sister Images: Guided Meditations from the Stories of Biblical Women*. Abingdon Press.